INITIATIVE

Human
and So

*The Hoover Institution
gratefully acknowledges
the generous support of*

JOANNE AND JOHAN BLOKKER

on this project.

INITIATIVE
Human Agency and Society

Tibor Machan

HOOVER INSTITUTION PRESS
Stanford University   Stanford, California

www.hoover.org

Hoover Institution Press Publication No. 468

First printing, 2000
06   05   04   03   02   01   00   9   8   7   6   5   4   3   2   1

Manufactured in the United States of America
The paper used in this publication meets the minimum requirements
of American National Standard for Information Sciences—Permanence
of Paper for Printed Library Materials, ANSI Z39.48–1984. ⊗

Library of Congress Cataloging-in-Publication Data
Machan, Tibor R.
    Initiative : human agency and society / Tibor R. Machan.
        p.   cm. — (Hoover Institution Press ; no. 468)
    Includes bibliographical references and index.
    ISBN 0-8179-9762-8
    1. Political ethics.   2. Policy sciences—Moral and ethical aspects.
3. Free will and determinism.   I. Title.   II. Hoover Institution Press
publication ; 468.
JA79 .M32   2000
1123′.5—dc21   99-049025

FOR THOMAS

Therefore, the proper work of man consists of living thoughtfully, in understanding, and in thoughtful action. The good life is the life that is in accordance with the natural order of man's being, the life that flows from a well-ordered or healthy soul. The good life simply, is the life in which the requirements of man's natural inclinations are fulfilled in the proper order to the highest possible degree, the life of a man who is awake to the highest possible degree, the life of a man in whose soul nothing lies waste.

—Leo Strauss, *Natural Right and History*, p. 127.

There's never been a problem yet I couldn't solve by thinking. I just don't usually choose to think.

—Tim Sandlin, *Sex and Sunsets*, p. 255.

CONTENTS

ACKNOWLEDGMENTS

I WISH TO THANK the editors of *To Be A Victim* (Plenum Publishing Co., 1991), *Liberty and the Rule of Law* (College Station: Texas A&M University Press, 1979), the *Journal of Applied Philosophy*, the *Partisan Review*, and the *Mid-Atlantic Journal of Business* for making it possible for me to use some of the work previously published in their forums. I also want to thank Randall R. Dipert, J. Roger Lee, and Mark Turiano for their help in my exploration of the ideas in this book. Roger E. Bissell, especially, prodded me with crucial objections and alternative ways of understanding the issues with which I tried to grapple. Jim Chesher was also very helpful in his thorough reading of and extensive comments on an initial draft of this work.

I also wish to thank John Raisian, director of the Hoover Institution, for his continued support of my work. Joanne and Johan Blokker's support of my work at the Hoover Institution is also gratefully acknowledged.

PREFACE

PUT PLAINLY, this book is about whether we can act on our own initiative and how it matters in politics and public policy. We seem to entertain contradictory views, both in the scholarly community and in our ordinary outlook on human affairs. We often blame or praise others and hold them and ourselves responsible for anything that we do, and we also often deny responsibility and culpability. These claims are not likely to be reconciled.

This book is addressed to educated lay people, calling attention to what's at stake and why the free will hypothesis, although often seemingly weak, is actually a strong one.

If we cannot act on our own initiative, then our behavior occurs independently of any original, creative (causal) influence by us. And then we live neither an ethically good nor a bad life and cannot be either blamed or praised. For ethics, as well as politics, is about what we do rightly or wrongly by our own choice, by our initiative. So there are no political wrongs, and our public officials cannot act other than they do. We cannot do anything about anything—it is all just phenomena unfolding inevitably. Choice is but a myth, maybe useful but unconnected with truth.

If, however, we possess the capacity to take the initiative—to determine on our own some of what we do—then we are responsible and often culpable when we act (unless we are crucially incapacitated). Ethics and law, which concern how we ought to or ought not to act and assume that the decision is ours in most cases, are then bona fide concerns of our lives.

In the history of human thought, mostly in philosophy and theology but also in psychology and some of the social sciences, this topic has been well discussed. Mostly, however, the treatment of it has been technical and esoteric. People not trained in the disciplines might become familiar with it in an introductory philosophy course, but otherwise the topic is not much attended to. Even in ethics courses and texts, specifically those in professional ethics, it is left unaddressed. Yet it is a vital one, and the implications of how we view it are everywhere in evidence—in personal relations, politics, criminal law, social work, and public policy.

To the question of whether we can do things on our own, the answer that I support is not revolutionary: Whether we *think* is up to us; we aren't forced to do it. From this freedom the rest follows, because actions depend mainly on judgments formed by our thinking. By means of the quality of our thinking, including our failure to think or to think enough, we are ultimately responsible for our conduct, for whether we do the right thing, get it more or less right, or act outright badly.[1]

I put the idea thus in a chapter of one of my recent books:

> Since thinking is the activity that is most directly under our own volition—we must activate it; no one can make us think (which, to a teacher, is all too evident)—what we must ultimately be blamed for has to be our failure to think. (Recall, again, the frequent exclamation, "Damn it, I didn't think!" upon having realized that one did the

1. I first came across this idea in Ayn Rand's novel *Atlas Shrugged* (New York: Random House, 1957). I later found the same idea in Aristotle, Aquinas, Spinoza, Locke, and Kant, although in somewhat different renditions.

wrong thing.) This is also the best way to understand the fact that morality is neither something wired into us nor something arbitrary.[2]

One reason many of us believe this, at least implicitly, most of the time is that even as we go about trying to address any topic or carrying on with various tasks in our lives, we consider some people's approaches sound and those of others less so. Even in a discussion such as the one in this book, a central issue is whether one is doing well or badly.

This suggests very strongly that our understanding of human conduct is infused with the belief that we act on our own initiative and are therefore responsible for what we do—in this case, how well or badly we think about the subject of personal initiative and moral responsibility.

But plain talk doesn't help us to grasp some unavoidable nuances and complexities; that is the reason for this book. I intend to avoid a terribly complicated, technical, and jargon-filled[3] investigation as much as possible, although some jargon may be necessary in some cases. Still, I want to develop an understanding of human initiative in a way that squares with common sense, science, and standards of philosophical clarity and to impress upon the reader the importance of the issue.

In numerous areas of very serious concern to us, confusions arise because it is unclear whether we possess the capacity to take the

2. Tibor R. Machan, *Classical Individualism* (London: Routledge, 1998), p. 47.

3. I should note that jargon is necessary within any bona fide specialty, since the more detailed exploration of phenomena produces concepts that to laypeople are more and more unfamiliar and remote. Bad jargon, of course, is a liability and often difficult for the layperson to detect. It consists of concepts that are ill formed, maybe even manufactured in order to help feign hard specialized work. But this need not be what jargon is all about. Concerning the topic at hand, perhaps the best collection of classic and contemporary essays is Derk Pereboom, ed., *Free Will* (Indianapolis, Ind.: Hackett Publishing Co., 1997). In this volume the position I find most convincing is laid out by Roderick Chisholm, "Human Freedom and the Self," pp. 143–55.

initiative at all, in any sphere of our behavior. In other words, there's doubt about whether we have free will, about whether can we be first causes as we go about living our lives, carrying out our various activities. Is what a criminal does ever something undertaken or initiated by him or her, or is the criminal always in some ever so subtle or blatant way driven or prodded to do the crime? And what of those who simply act impolitely or are very brave? Are they individually responsible for such conduct? or have they been impelled by their genetic makeup or environmental stimuli, or both, to behave as they did?

The bulk of the law and morality rests on the assumption that human beings have free will and can initiate their conduct, that what they do is up to them. They are held responsible for good and bad deeds because they did them of their own initiative. Yet, in the social sciences, especially, as well as in popular forums, many doubts are raised about this: Could we not, in fact, explain everything people do by reference to various causes, contingencies, variables, laws of nature, and so forth, provided we know the relevant factors involved? Is our behavior not, in fact, caused by various forces working on us, producing what we do, so that if we could only discover them all, our behavior could be fully explained with no need for any such notion as personal initiative, free choice, or personal responsibility?

Psychologists, sociologists, economists, and many others often proceed as if they could find complete explanations for human action without any reference to the person's own initiative as a causal force. Scholars in the field of law and economics, for example, insist that when institutions arise in different societies, regardless of how varied they are, there is always some explanation by reference, as they put it, to someone's interest. Church rituals, wars, artifacts, developments in science and industry—in every case it is at least in principle possible to discover what impels people to behave as they do. Someone must have been getting something out of it, and that aim itself is a biological or genetic drive, not a matter of individual initiative. In other human and social sciences (e.g., psychology, anthropology, sociology, economics) the source of explanation may differ—some invoke the laws of genetics, some utility maximization, others the survival instinct or peer pressure. It is either nature or nurture or some combination of both, but in any case what we do is supposedly produced by factors causing our behavior, not by us as decisive causal agents.[4]

The following report will reinfoirce the nature of the problem:

> Consider Harvard's most popular science class, Human Behavioral Biology. Nicknamed "Sex" by students, the course seeks to provide a scientific understanding of human behavior through an approach mixing biological evolution, anthropology, neuroscience, psychology and linguistics. The first lecture of the class began with a slide of Bill Clinton, provoking titters from the crowd. His adultery was offered as an example of behavior soon to be explained as a product of various developmental, functional, mechanistic, and evolutionary causes. The course was judicious in discounting both strict biological and environmental determinism. But the notion of free will with its attendant moral responsibilities was given short shrift.[5]

Among many philosophers, also, the idea that we are impelled to behave as we do is widely accepted, although in such cases the notion is also advanced that such impulsion does not void human freedom but is, in fact, required by it.[6]

4. The language of "causation" is sometimes traded in for talk of "variables" that account for what we do. As an example, a recent work, Adam Kuper, *Culture: The Anthropologists' Account* (Cambridge, Mass.: Harvard University Press, 1999) makes the case against cultural determinism. It argues, as the advertisement of the book announces, that "political and economic forces, social institutions, and biological process must take their place in any complete explanation of why people think and behave as they do." It is noteworthy that the one agent left out of the proposed complete explanation is the individual person!

5. Roman Martinez, "Notebook," *The New Criterion*, March 1999.

6. A very detailed and intricate development of this "compatibilist" view may be found in Irving Thalberg, *Enigmas of Agency* (London: George Allen and Unwin, 1972). One reason such a view is very appealing may be that it seems to its proponents the only way to save a coherent naturalism, namely, by not exempting human conduct

When biological determinism is contested in prominent forums, it is not because human agency is seen to have a role. For example, Philip Yam states that "Biology is not destiny and the environment that shapes our motivations and passions is crucial to a fulfilled life."[7] This strongly suggests that, in opposition to genetic or biological determinism, the only alternative is environmental determinism. So, as the current debate lines up on the topic, it must be either biological or environmental determinants (or some combination of the two) that fuel a fulfilled life. The agency or initiative of the human individual is not even considered.

Stephen Hawking, the world-famous theoretical physicist, put the matter this way: "In summary, the title of this essay was a question: is everything determined? The answer is yes, it is. But it might as well not be, because we can never know what is determined."[8] In his opinion it is our lack of adequate knowledge, an inherent uncertainty, that leads to the view that everything "might as well not be" determined. In fact, however, he believes that everything is—and there are those who know this. So our actions are not free. We are not capable of bona fide choice, of taking the initiative, but must yield to the force of the causes impinging upon us. The old picture, modeled on how a billiard ball comes to move as it does, holds many of us captive, probably because it appears that letting go of it implies a random, erratic, lawless universe.

Apart from the academic disciplines of the various sciences and engineering, members of the general public now often believe, at least

---

from what is taken to be the force that reigns uniformly throughout nature: causality. However, as noted already, this assumes that causality takes only one form, that of efficient causation, and that agent causation is not a valid form of it. This idea is just what is disputed in this book, as well as in others that advance a naturalist account of bona fide free will or human initiative.

7. Philip Yam, "Clean Genes," *Scientific American* (October 1997): 154.
8. Stephen Hawking, *Black Holes and Baby Universes and Other Essays* (New York: Bantam Books, 1993), p. 126.

implicitly, that we act because we are forced to by circumstances. A television news anchor introduces a segment on a program by saying, "What made this man behave as he did when he risked his life?" It isn't "Why did the man act as he did?"—in which case the answer might be, "This was his choice; he acted this way out of conviction, self-determination or self-discipline." Rather it is assumed that some causes drove him to behave as he did.

As far as freedom is concerned, some people think that what human beings do just happens randomly, without anyone's having caused it and being responsible for it. For example, when in the fall of 1997 a disgruntled 67-year-old man, Carl Drega—"a local recluse nursing a twisted grudge over his property rights"—killed four people in the United States and then was himself gunned down, John Harrigan, publisher of the local paper, the *News and Sentinel* of Colebrook, New Hampshire, observed: "He was just a piece of space junk that happened to get us."[9] Some scholars who believe in what has come to be called libertarianism match this view that human behavior is indeterminate, even random (perhaps because of the influence of the alleged randomness of the behavior of subatomic particles).[10] Steven Pinker's position backs up this outlook on free will. He thinks there is a sense of the concept of "free will," namely, one consistent with science based on speculations about chaos in the brain. Yet Pinker also seems to subscribe to the Kantian idea that "Science and morality are separate spheres of reasoning. Only by recognizing them as separate can we have them both."[11] Pinker made the following observation,

9. *New York Times*, October 17, 1997, p. A16.

10. John Eccles and Sir Karl Popper, *The Self and Its Brain* (New York: Springer-Verlag, 1977). The earliest statement of this view is perhaps found in Lucretius's *On the Nature of Things*, ed., Anthony M. Esolen (Baltimore: Johns Hopkins University Press, 1995). See Pereboom, *Free Will*, for the relevant sections.

11. Steven Pinker, Letter to the Editors, *Washington Post* (from http://www-bcs.mit.edu/~steve/washpost.html). In his book *How the Mind Works* (New York:

which is quite consistent with the above quote and assessment of his position:

> There are two very different senses of free will—a scientific sense, in which some behaviors are not, and may never be, predictable, presumably because they originate in noise, chaos, or quantum effects in the brain. Then there's a moral sense, in which some behaviors are not considered to be caused at all, and the person is held morally responsible for them. I think it's important to keep them distinct (so that we don't excuse more and more evil behavior the more we understand the brain). I also think we are unlikely ever to understand the relation between the scientific and moral versions, because our minds are not designed to grasp the moral concept of free will fully.[12]

My answer as follows helps to set the stage for this book:

> I hold out hope that if free will or self-determination is a fact, it must be something completely compatible with other facts, i.e., science. I cannot fathom a basic conflict between our nature and the way the world generally must work, so to speak. This is why I found the [Roger W.] Sperry line very fruitful—he is close to how Spinoza and Aristotle (or Aristotelians) tend to deal with this matter.[13]

In the majority of cases brain scientists seem to hold—and even with Pinker this may be implicit—that once enough of the facts are known, it will be possible to say which factors have caused what occurred. And there will be no need to invoke anything like personal initiative or agency.

Even if it is not possible, the reason is not that human initiative

---

W. W. Norton, 1997), Pinker explains that he does not deny free will but considers it a kind of mystery that must be dealt with apart from science.

12. Personal communication, November 22, 1997.
13. Personal communication, November 22, 1997.

plays a decisive role but that an epistemological law of uncertainty renders getting hold of all the causal factors impossible. For the time being, Pinker seems to settle for a fundamental mysteriousness about the human mind, involving, in Colin McGinn's terms, "sentience, the self, free will, meaning, knowledge, morality."[14] Furthermore, as McGinn notes in his review of Pinker's book, "To have nothing to say about the nature and the function of consciousness in a book purporting to tell us how the mind works strikes me as, let us say, a gap."[15]

Yet, of course, much is said in favor of human initiative in natural enough terms, at least implicitly. Employers often look for employees who are self-starters. Parents are held responsible for failing, on their own accord, to treat their children as they deserve. People in similar circumstances are taken to carry on differently because they have decided of their own free will to do so. Artists create original works open to criticism or at least evaluation. Scientists forge new understandings but are also involved in fraud and the misapplication of their findings. Adolescents reject what they are offered by their elders and insist on inventing new fashions, entertainment, and so forth, which is often unwise and imprudent of them to do.

The world is filled with what human beings produce for no other reason than that they thought up the idea. They are held responsible for this both ethically and legally. Thus, clearly, we treat one another as if we could take the initiative, if only in our discussing various topics. When, furthermore, Ted Honderich concluded his championing of determinism in his book *How Free Are You?*, wondering, "should one part of the response of affirmation be a move to the Left in politics" because free will does not exist, he inadvertently assumed that we

---

14. Colin McGinn, "The Know-It-All" (review of *How the Mind Works*, by Steven Pinker), *New Republic* (February 23, 1998): 37.

15. Ibid., p. 38.

have a choice as to whether we should make that move, that we could take the initiative either way.[16]

I submit that free will is a feature of our natural, biological nature and needs to be accounted for not by invoking the mysterious but by finding a place for it within the framework of a naturalist understanding of human life. As one biologist writing on the topic of biological determinism put it, "our freedom is inherent in the living processes that constitute us."[17]

So then, what is the answer? Are we able to take the initiative as far as our conduct is concerned? Or is free will a myth to be wisely discarded? In short, are we responsible for any of our significant actions? Are we doing some important things of our own initiative? Are certain matters actually up to us? Or is initiative an illusion, as B. F. Skinner maintained about freedom of the will when he recommended moving "beyond freedom and dignity"?[18]

One reason I chose to deal with the issue is that I am not satisfied with how some of the most prominent theorists have dealt with it. This book might be thought of as an attempt to transcend the Kantian bifurcation of the scientific and moral realms of reality and human life. Indeed, it seems there is a desperate demand for doing so, given how these two realms are constantly interfacing in ethics, law, politics, and international diplomacy. Moral and legal guilt are both diminished in some prominent schools of psychiatry and psychology. Public policy, in turn, is forged both by social scientists and by the moral attitudes of voters and politicians. The fate of developing nations rests, in large measure, on how scientific and ethical conceptions contribute to guiding them—one need but consider the influence of concerns about

16. Ted Honderich, *How Free Are You?* (Oxford: Oxford University Press, 1993), p. 129.

17. Steven Rose, *Lifeline: Biology beyond Determinism* (London: Oxford University Press, 1998), p. 6.

18. B. F. Skinner, *Beyond Freedom and Dignity* (New York: Bantam Books, 1972).

human rights violations on matters of commerce and scientific cooperation among diverse countries of the world.

To leave the inquiry with the claim that the scientific and the ethical are simply irreconcilable is to accept defeat concerning our efforts to understand our kind of life on earth.

Recalling Kant, we might say that this book is designed to be a step toward reintegrating or debifurcating the phenomenal and noumenal aspects of reality—an apologist of Aristotle responding to Kant, perhaps.

My task here will be to show, in various contexts, that free will exists, that human beings have the capacity to initiate their own conduct. My approach will involve what may appear to be excessive repetition. This is necessary so as to demonstrate over and over again, in the course of discussing the various aspects of the topic itself, that human beings cannot *reasonably* deny that they are free.

I hope that making the point in various contexts, relating it to economics, science, ethics, politics, and arguing about the topic itself, will help bring it home effectively and convincingly. If some of it seems redundant it is because there are many hurdles to overcome and the point must be shown to hold in however many contexts we might be tempted to deny it.

Law and Ethics and Initiative

No one could know the heart of darkness that impelled them
[Ted Bundy and Jeffrey Dahmer] to commit their crimes.
—Mike Wallace, *Twentieth Century* (A&E)

IS INITIATIVE NECESSARY for at least the criminal law and for ethics? Yes.[1] To start with, I argue that the insight of Immanuel Kant, that "'ought' implies 'can'" is inescapable. Assume that to say that someone ought to do such and such is to mean something substantive. That is to say, it expresses something that is true and is not used only to prod people to do things, to give them encouragement or an incen-

---

1. I have explored a number of crucial works in this area and found either no mention or barely a hint concerning whether human beings possess free will. See, for example, Alan Goldman, *The Moral Foundations of Professional Ethics* (Totowa, N.J.: Rowman and Littlefield, 1980); Albert Flores, ed., *Professional Ideals* (Belmont, Calif.: Wadsworth Publishing Co., 1988); Nicholas Fotion and Gerard Elfstrom, *Military Ethics* (London: Routledge and Kegan Paul, 1986); Lloyd J. Matthews and Dale E. Brown, eds., *The Parameters of Military Ethics* (New York: Pergamon-Brassey's, 1989), and Darrell Reeck, *Ethics for the Professions: A Christian Perspective* (Minneapolis, Minn.: Augsburg Publishing House, 1982). The same holds in both the general and the specialized applied ethics works, as well as journal papers.

tive to behave in certain ways.[2] Then the person must have the capacity to do either what he ought or what he ought not.

This surely is still the default position of the criminal law: Normally a convicted rapist is taken to have been capable of acting so as not to commit the crime. In other words, at some point the person could have acted other than he did in committing the rape. Some comply when they are told "no"; others do not but proceed to commit the rape. However, they did not have to do it; it was not unavoidable; they were not compelled to do it by anyone or anything.

Thus the criminal is responsible for having done the crime that the law assumes he might not have done had he made the right choice. There are, however, two different ways to argue against this. First, as Clarence Darrow argued, the criminal law is obsolete, simply mistaken, in the grips of what B. F. Skinner called "prescientific" notions. Second, what it means to say "he ought to have done otherwise than he did" is not that he actually could have done otherwise but something else—that it would have been best for all concerned had he done otherwise. As to any punishment for such deeds, it amounts to a means of discouragement or deterrent, not a response to a wrong choice. (Or by "wrong choice" we must mean no more than that what the person

2. It is often argued by skeptics about free will that all of the language of ethics, morality, law, and so forth can be understood in this behaviorist fashion. They argue that it does not amount to something true about what people ought or ought not to do, as if they had a choice. Rather it will simply induce them to behave in certain ways, to set before them additional possibilities and to goad them to select the one that is deemed of value to them. And it is denied, then, that "ought" implies "can" in the sense that if one ought to do X, then one is free to do either X or non-X. Clearly, however, that is not what we take statements with "ought" to mean.

Moreover, the language of blaming and praising is said by the critics to have little use. It accomplishes nothing. To this, those who take free will seriously will respond by noting that whether it works to change behavior is not the point of giving praise or blame. Rather, the point is to state something true, namely, that one has done something correctly and morally, or not. That in itself is important—that the action is intended not to produce some effect but to register a fact, an action that may, but may well not, have some desired effect.

did turned out badly, all things considered.) When people are "impelled" by "the heart of darkness," they aren't acting on their own initiative. They are pushed to do wrong.

I do not think either of these options succeeds. By this I mean they are very probably false. And that, in turn, means that the facts known to us cannot be adequately understood by such a rendering of the nature of either crime or morality.

Also, in the context of widespread social scientism, silence on this topic of whether human beings have the capacity to initiate some of their crucial conduct amounts to acquiescence to or at least tolerance of the deterministic view of human behavior. That is the idea in terms of which individual moral responsibility, thus ethics or law, is precluded from human affairs, private or public (or reinterpreted in ways that no longer acknowledge the moral dimension of human existence).

The matter cannot be resolved by ignoring it.[3] And fortunately there is now renewed interest in addressing the issue, although not always with sufficient detail and perseverance—the cognitive sciences, psycholinguistics, brain–mind studies, and so forth, tend, in the main, to shun the issue of human initiative. Most troublesome is the fact that ethics—especially in the applied specialties such as

---

3. Ernst Haeckel argued this in the nineteenth century. As I discuss in chapter 1, the widely published moral philosopher John Kekes believes that freedom is simply lack of coercion. Jan Narveson also appears to think, judging from our e-mail exchanges, that the free-will issue is a bogus one and suggests that all that matters is whether one is acting uncoerced by someone else. If one does, one is free in the only relevant practical sense of that term. As Narveson puts it, "The 'metaphysical question of free will,' as I call it, remains of interest, but I think it is abstract interest, not practical interest. I continue to think that it can make no difference whatever to practice" (personal communication, January 29, 1999). In my view, this is a mistake. How we relate to others has much to do with whether they are free agents. Clearly, if a dog had free will, we would probably charge the dog with assault for biting the mailman rather than charging its owner with negligence. For more on this, see chapter 3.

business, engineering, medicine, and so forth—is discussed without taking into consideration its connection to free will.

In support of the initiative idea, there is, to begin with, no end of blaming and praising going on in both the academic and the nonacademic worlds in our time. In applied ethics, in particular, persons in the professions of medicine, law, business, science, and education are said to have certain responsibilities. They are to conduct themselves in prescribed ways and to abstain from various negative kinds of conduct. Often very serious lawsuits rest on claims of what such people have done or failed to do, as for example when tobacco companies are attacked. (Oddly, although smokers are often said to have no free will either to take up their habit or to quit—because advertising makes them do the former, and addiction prevents them from doing the latter—the companies are deemed free and responsible for their conduct, answerable for what they did! Of course, their attorneys could invoke some theory as to their having been compelled—by something in their history, such as their training in business school—to market a product hazardous to our health.)

Claims about accountability, liability, responsibility, and ethics in general are made in textbooks, treatises, and academic journals, as well as in the general media. Also, in the case of such issues as AIDS research, gun control, civil rights bills, entitlement programs, and so forth, we find that numerous academicians enter the fray as moralizers, by means of radio and television appearances and newspaper columns, as well as articles in prestigious magazines. This is especially true during political elections. And such moralizing would not make much sense if people simply had to act as they do and choices were irrelevant to the story.

Many scholars contribute to discussion of such moral matters, often in the lay media—for example, in the capacity of what are now called ethicists! This is especially so when cases involving what are called ethical dilemmas make front page news, such as assisted suicides, surrogate mothering, euthanasia, testing for the AIDS virus, accidents attributed to drug abuse, racially motivated violence, and so forth.

On the other hand, we also find that many laypeople, apart from scholars in various fields, identify their own misbehavior in nonmoral terms, avoiding the language of blaming and praising. As already noted, in academic social science human behavior is treated primarily as an effect of causes over which individuals have no control—their upbringing, genetic makeup, economic class membership, cultural background, and so forth. In the fields of psychology, economics, sociology, anthropology, and political science, many of the prominent modes of analysis and explanation subscribe to some version of the nature/nurture deterministic framework, with no theoretical room left for individual self-determination that is not reducible to some outside or built-in forces.

Furthermore, the lay media abounds in discussion of different types of addiction, so that some of the most lamentable conduct by people is deemed to be a result of an affliction or a disease. There are in this view no drunks but merely victims of alcoholism; there are no philanderers or adulterers, only the sex addicted. Drug abusers, as well as heavy smokers, are classified as suffering from addiction; people who are overweight or undernourished or abusive toward their children or their spouses, are identified as suffering from some condition that is supposed to explain this behavior in full.

CONFUSION AND INJUSTICE
BASED ON INCONSISTENCY

The practical consequences of such a divided outlook, whereby much of the discussion in the culture both condemns and exonerates individuals when it comes to their lamentable conduct, may well be confusion, as well as injustice. If in order to act effectively—including establishing institutions to guide long-range behavior and policies—people must have ideas by which to be guided, and if these ideas imply conflicting, even contradictory, courses of action, it seems reasonable to expect much confusion and even injustice to arise.[4] We come to understand ourselves in one of the following two ways: either as capable of being individually responsible for many problems in our lives or as unable to act by our own judgment.

In this light, we must see ourselves as divided in a rather fundamental way. Such division, if justified, would discourage efforts toward resolving problems, ironing out differences, solving apparent contradictions. We would at best be advised to just accept the surrounding confusion and live within a world in which blaming and praising continue side by side with the conviction that no one can help doing whatever it is he or she is doing, because it is all a matter of an ongoing procession of causal connections.

This confusion also engenders the serious vulnerability in many in our culture to making opportunistic moralistic attacks—harsh scolding and finger wagging—which are themselves excused by appealing to environmental, genetic, economic, cultural, and other forms of determinism. Outbursts, denunciations, and so forth, are often discussed in this fashion—for example, on talk shows, as well as in more serious social commentaries. People angrily attack others but then excuse themselves on the grounds that they cannot help themselves, not realizing that those at whom they are angry are subject to the same excuse and thus undeserving of the scolding being dished out.

And it seems that philosophers contribute amply to this problematic situation. Such views as compatibilism seem to suggest that although no one can act other than in the one way he or she has been compelled to act, nonetheless responsibility for the act and its consequences may coherently be assigned to the agent. This view has surface appeal because it preserves the prevalent determinism many sci-

---

4. The injustice would arise only if the confusion were a result of culpable negligence. Yet, of course, the problem we are exploring is itself whether the very idea of injustice can be made sense of within the widespread confusion that abounds.

entifically minded people insist on as they seek to understand the world while making room for the well-entrenched, seemingly indispensable evaluative judgments they make concerning how people behave.

Yet are people morally responsible even if they could not make a decisive difference in their own conduct? Can it be that a person ought or should do or have done something even though there is nothing else he or she could do or have done? Those questions are just the sort in need of greater attention.[5]

All the talk of responsibility, guilt, regret, and morality itself has, of course, been dismissed along lines heard from the late psychologist B. F. Skinner. He urged that such talk is merely uninformed, based on folk psychology, which is little more than myth and has by now been eclipsed by the findings of modern science.[6] Others dismiss it in more circumspect ways, such as by claiming that science and morality are different spheres, with reason an effective tool of inquiry in the former but only faith and mystery surrounding the latter. That, too, poses puzzles because, if reason cannot deal with some subject matter, we are, as rational animals, pretty much barred from understanding it.

So we are hardly confined to cases involving the remarks and conduct of presumably uninitiated laypeople. There is ample material from the forums in which professional philosophers and other scholars

5. It is interesting to observe that already at this point of our discussion what has been termed "the determinist's dilemma" confronts us—namely, could such lamentations even make sense concerning human behavior, including forming a belief in certain propositions, unless individuals had the capacity and power to undertake to change their conduct of their own accord? See James N. Jordan, "Determinism's Dilemma," *Review of Metaphysics* 23 (September 1969): 48–66.

6. B. F. Skinner, *Beyond Freedom and Dignity* (New York: Bantam Books, 1972). I have discussed Skinner's views in Tibor R. Machan, *The Pseudo-Science of B. F. Skinner* (New Rochelle, N.Y.: Arlington House, 1974).

hold forth. There, too, praising and blaming (and its cognates[7]) are as frequent as anywhere else.

In our time applied ethics—parental, fraternal, and professional (e.g., medical, business, legal, engineering, educational)—is a flourishing field. Philosophers and others, often called ethicists, who have at times considerable legal clout make claims about how doctors, lawyers, politicians, soldiers, business managers, personnel directors, teachers, parents, and men and women fulfilling innumerable other roles in life ought or ought not to act. Journals abound in many varieties of applied ethics (as well as in the broader fields of social and political philosophy and public policy), with most papers featuring judgments as to what people in these fields ought or ought not do. Alternatively, we are told what laws or rules legislators or regulators ought to enact so as to compel such professionals to behave properly.[8]

Perhaps even more basically, though, all of philosophical scholarship—indeed, all scholarship—contains the normative dimension of criticism and evaluation. It implies, clearly, that the authors believe those who are the targets of their criticisms ought to have perceived more carefully and reasoned differently from how they did. That, too,

---

7. Arguably philosophers express their praise and blame somewhat subtly, not always using the most direct terms to signify blaming or praising. (Consider when philosophers criticize one another on grounds of logic alone—that kind of comment, too, invokes certain norms that presumably the target of criticism ought to heed!) Moreover, we may without any distortion include within our class of beliefs and utterances various proclamations concerning what people ought or ought not to do and what sort of conduct and practices by persons and human organizations or institutions should or should not be carried out.

8. Not just journals but also textbooks, conferences, and university courses proliferate that feature claims as to what various professionals ought or ought not to do. And, of course, philosophers are active in the various controversies about multiculturalism, feminism, freedom of expression, and so forth that abound on university campuses; so here, too, they immerse themselves in ethics and need to be clear about whether they are addressing themselves to human beings who can make free choices or who are being moved about by forces over which they cannot exert any independent, original control.

suggests that they hold to some version of the position that human beings are fundamentally capable of making basic choices and of taking the initiative to act one way or another and are responsible for how they do act.

THE PHILOSOPHER'S ROLE

Given all such moralizing from professional philosophers and many others, it is curious if not outright scandalous—assuming such a moral notion does have a place in rational discourse—how little attention is paid to whether we have the capacity for initiative outside some special segments of the philosophical community. This is especially difficult to accept regarding work in applied ethics, since in that area philosophers aren't dealing with the highly abstract issue of how ethics might be justified, which ethical system is sound, and so forth, but with how we should conduct ourselves in various spheres of human activity. In applied ethics we ask whether human beings are equipped to direct or guide themselves so that they can be held responsible for how they act, for whether they do what is right or what is wrong in their various roles. How can we worry about corporate social responsibility or accountability by politicians and bureaucrats, let alone parents and teachers, if all proceeds as it must and no one can make choices and act differently from how they in fact do? Why bother about proper versus improper relations between a president and a White House intern if no one can initiate his or her conduct, if all things just happen to us?

There is then a widely admitted and apparently quite sound philosophical idea that "'ought' implies 'can,'" especially in circumstances not fraught with paradox.[9] So it seems odd that many philosophers

---

9. Some, such as John Kekes, argue that there can be exceptions to this idea. See John Kekes, "'Ought Implies Can' and Kinds of Morality," *Philosophical Quarterly* 34 (1984): 460–67. See also his *Facing Evil* (Princeton, N.J.: Princeton University

especially and other students of human life are not eager to reconcile all their moralizing and criticizing with their views of human nature and motivation.[10] Shouldn't there be a national debate about this? Isn't it vital whether a Theodore Kaczinsky is treated as a criminal or some kind of a virus, or Stalin and Hitler as natural calamities or moral monsters?

Here I first explore why no great effort has been made in much of contemporary philosophy to draw together the normative and ontological aspects of substantive moral or ethical theorizing in our time. Again, there isn't total silence on the relationship between ethics and human nature, specifically whether human individuals can be original causes or initiators of their actions. But these discussions are not conducted in those forums in which most of the substantive applied ethical analysis is carried out, nor by those who focus most intensely on substantive ethics. Indeed, it is these same applied ethicists who seem not to touch on the issue of individual responsibility and allow us to assess how they square their moral exhortations with some compatible view of human nature. After all, what can be made of applied ethics, or indeed any ethics, if the best science tells us that we are fully determined to behave as we do? If the answer to the question, Is everything determined? is Yes, it is, what does it matter whether doctors, politicians, educators, merchants, bankers, diplomats, or other professionals misbehave? There is nothing that can be done about it by anyone.

And so ethics comes to naught but, to echo Hamlet, "There is nothing either good or bad, but thinking makes it so."[11] Our values are

---

Press, 1991), which includes the bulk of the discussion from the aforementioned paper as well as such other papers as "Freedom," *Pacific Philosophical Quarterly* 61 (1980): 368–85.

10. Not that some philosophers do not worry about the matter. But they are not among those who contribute to the various burgeoning subfields of applied ethics.

11. William Shakespeare, *Hamlet*, act 2, scene 2, line 259. *The Works of William Shakespeare* (Secaucus, N.J.: Castle, n.d.), p. 340.

of our making, since what is good is not so much a discovery but an expression of our feelings. Discovering the good presupposes the knowability and objectivity of what is good. But only what science can affirm via empirical methods can qualify for such existence—all the work by David Hume and G. E. Moore points that way, in part because they were both empiricists and determinists.

THE GENESIS OF DISJOINTEDNESS

To begin with, let us make note of the fact that much of the energy and activity in moral philosophy in public policy was started with the work of John Rawls, whose book *A Theory of Justice*[12] certainly launched a renewal of political philosophy, as well as a good deal of moral philosophy, in the Anglo-American tradition. (Robert Nozick's work[13] did not seriously challenge this approach, nor did earlier works in this genre[14]).

Yet this resurrection came with an expensive proviso, attached explicitly by John Rawls in his presidential address, "The Independence of Moral Theory," given before the American Philosophical Association in 1974.[15] Rawls's thesis was that we need to forget about the grand, systematic philosophical projects and attend only to questions of morality. As Rawls put it, a "relation of methodological priority does not hold, I believe, between the theory of meaning, epistemology, and the philosophy of mind on the one hand and moral philosophy on the other. To the contrary: a central part of moral philosophy is what I have called moral theory; it consists in the comparative study of moral

12. Cambridge, Mass.: Harvard University Press, 1971.

13. *Anarchy, State, and Utopia* (New York: Basic Books, 1974).

14. Brian Barry, *Political Arguments* (London: Routledge and Kegan Paul, 1965), Nicholas Rescher, *Distributive Justice* (New York: Bobbs-Merrill, 1966).

15. *Proceedings and Addresses of the American Philosophical Association*, vol. 47 (Newark, Del.: American Philosophical Association, 1975), pp. 5–22.

conceptions, which is, in large part, independent."[16] Thus ethics, morality, and public policy were to be approached without what used to be called "philosophical foundations."

In a way, Rawls's thesis echoed several decades of ordinary language and analytic philosophy that had been antagonistic toward system building. It was, furthermore, just another turn away from the kind of moral theorizing that had been attacked by David Hume in his *Treatise of Human Nature* several centuries ago. System building was once more declared to be useless and philosophically unjustified. Philosophy was supposed to scale down its scope and become more piecemeal. We were to look at various issues that had been the province of philosophy in isolation from philosophical thinking. Exactly how the recategorization of such traditional philosophical issues was to happen was a matter of the different methodologies and theories of the various competing schools. But, though competing, these schools had tended to agree on one fundamental principle: that philosophy was impotent when it came to such questions as, What is the nature of knowledge and moral knowledge? and What is the nature of the good and the moral good? Even such questions as, Do human being possess freedom of will? is there a God? and so forth, were deemed by many to be out of bounds for philosophical investigations.

We may fairly associate these attitudes with subschools of empiricism, logical positivism, linguistic analysis, ordinary language philosophy, pragmatism, existentialism, and so forth.[17] Rawls's indepen-

---

16. Ibid., p. 21.

17. Of course, these general schools divide into many subsections based on innumerable refinements of the main features of these broadly characterized schools. Some of them may not agree with the position I ascribe to them above. Yet there need be little argument about this here, for in their central claims these views do find it unlikely, if not outright impossible, for philosophy proper to handle normative, especially ethical and political, problems. Exceptions to these orientations have always existed, though perhaps not in the most prominent centers of academic philosophy and ethics. See, for example, the work of W. D. Falk, collected in his book, *Ought, Reasons, and Morality* (Ithaca, N.Y.: Cornell University Press, 1986).

dence of moral theory thesis was another way of putting essentially the same point: Ethics, philosophy of law, political philosophy, public policy issues, and the like were all to be handled on the basis of impressions, intuitions, what seems to make the best sense under ordinary circumstances and in ordinary terms, and so forth, placed, of course, in a "reflective equilibrium."[18] Following Rawls's own work, as well as Nozick's partial endorsement of its methodology—since Nozick, too, used ordinary intuitions to test the feasibility of his assumed natural rights—a great number of articles began to appear in journals such as *Ethics*, *Philosophy and Public Affairs*, and *Social Theory and Practice*, in which this independence of moral theory thesis was assumed to be correct, and moral discussions were conducted accordingly.[19]

STARTING WITH INTUITIONS

Evidence for this point may be gleaned from the fact that these articles usually begin with an assertion concerning "our considered moral judgments" or "moral intuitions" and then proceed to sketch out some kind of a derivation as it applies to an area of public policy, morality, law, and politics. It is arguable, however, that this tactic is misguided.[20] One consideration that had to be neglected, in consequence of such "independence," is whether any of this moral and

18. One may suppose that this provision is part of the process so as to avoid total arbitrariness, which intuitionism per se would entail. Yet there is reason to think that introducing the proviso robs the method of its independence. See Tibor R. Machan, "A Note on Independence," *Philosophical Studies* 30 (1976): 419–21.

19. These are only the most prestigious of the ethics and public affairs journals. We can also include *The Journal of Value Inquiry*, *Business and Professional Ethics Journal*, *The Journal of Business Ethics*, and *Environmental Ethics*, in which this practice still prevails. Obviously, there have also been exceptions. But the connection between substantive ethical claims and the topic of free will is rarely explored, as indicated by the works listed in note 1.

20. I did, in fact, so argue in Machan, "A Note on Independence."

political exhortation had a realistic base in human nature, in the nature of the being that is the intended audience of such discussions—especially when it comes to readers of textbooks and collections of case analyses. How can we engage in redistribution of wealth, why ought we to strive for the equal treatment of everyone in a society, why should we abstain from sexual discrimination and harassment, from insider trading, tax evasion, exploitative or imperialistic foreign trade or policies, or greedy financial scheming if, in fact, we can't help what we do, if we are moved by forces over which we have no control?

Philosophers may not have outright endorsed the view B. F. Skinner placed on record—although John Rawls himself came extremely close to doing just that when he wrote that a person's "character depends in large part upon fortunate family and social circumstances for which he can claim no credit."[21] However, their colleagues within academe in the social sciences, including economists, sociologists, psychologists, anthropologists, and others, have mostly formulated theories that discount free human agency as regards our conduct, institutions, and laws.[22]

Assume it turns out that there is no way for us to do anything but what we must do, as determined by the neural powers, the mechanics of our brain, the socioeconomic conditions that have surrounded us

21. Rawls, *A Theory of Justice*, p. 104. Incidentally, if this view is not a kind of metaethical position, not much else would qualify. In light of Rawls's "independence" thesis, it is difficult to see why he can rest any beliefs on it. Furthermore, once the topic is broached, it would be instructive to see what exactly Rawls's view on it is—to wit, if it is "in large part" that character depends on circumstances, what little bit of self-responsibility is it proper for us to expect human beings to have and how is it to be accounted for in understanding ethics and public policy matters?

22. I discuss some of this in greater detail in Tibor R. Machan, "Rescuing Victims—from Social Theory," in Diane Sank and David I. Caplan, eds., *To Be a Victim: Encounters with Crime and Injustice* (New York: Plenum Press, 1991), pp. 101–16. See also Tibor R. Machan, *Capitalism and Individualism* (New York: St. Martin's Press, 1990), for a discussion of the impact of the social scientistic position of economists on their explorations of which of the various live competing political economic options has the greatest merit as a system of human community life.

during our "formative" years, or some similar candidate. Assume, in other words, that the deterministic conception of human nature is correct. Assume, furthermore, that no fundamental challenge to this essentially mechanistic model of the human mind and consciousness has been prominently advanced—and there certainly has not been such a challenge in much of nineteenth- and twentienth-century philosophy.[23] If all this is accepted, especially by those engaged in the promulgation of moral and political ideals, one can certainly wonder how anyone is to make any sense of the claim that people ought to do or abstain from doing the myriad things that moral philosophers, public policy analysts, and political philosophers maintain that they should.

THE IMPORTANCE OF HAVING INITIATIVE

First, let me outline my argument in defense of human initiative or free will, that is, that human beings can cause some of what they do

---

23. The mechanistic model allows for nuanced differences based on highly technical amendments to the broad framework contributed by, say, quantum physics. Yet that will not change the basic result, namely, that self-responsibility is disallowed and, thus, ethics rendered impossible.

Of course, challenges exist—for example, those advanced by Karl Popper and John C. Eccles in *The Self and Its Brain* (New York: Springer International, 1977) and John C. Eccles, *Evolution of the Brain: Creation of the Self* (London: Routledge, 1989). Popper and Eccles argue that quantum mechanics makes room for free will in some fashion, although they seem to adopt a new dualism, reminiscent of Kant's project. The effort has not met with much approval within the community of philosophers, let alone moral and public policy theorists. Part of the problem is that quantum mechanics, especially the Heisenberg uncertainty principle, does not provide ethics with a metaphysical but only a pseudoepistemological grounding, leading to the possible result that randomness is part of the universe. This is not at all the same as self-responsibility.

In social scientific circles, too, there have been dissenters, such as Isidor Chein, *The Science of Behavior and the Image of Man* (New York: Basic Books, 1972), and Nathaniel Branden, *The Psychology of Self-Esteem* (New York: Bantam Books, 1969). It is fair to note, however, that these did not make an impact in applied ethics.

on their own. In other words, what human beings do is not explainable solely by references to factors that have influenced them but must include reference to their own causal agency or initiative.

I shall later develop the argument in greater detail. For now I merely wish to give a sketchy rendition of my thesis that human beings are able to cause their actions and that they are therefore responsible for some of them. In a basic sense we are all original actors capable of making novel moves in the world. We are, in other words, initiators of some of our behavior.

The first matter to be noted is that the suggestion that free will exists in no way contradicts science. Initiative could well be a natural phenomenon, something that emerged in nature with the emergence of human beings who have minds that can think and be aware of their own thinking. In other words, that some animals might be facilitated to be original and creative, rather than largely reflexive, responsive, or reactive, is not ipso facto a violation of the laws of nature.

Nature is complicated and multifaceted. It includes many different sorts of things, and one of these is human beings. Such beings may well exhibit one unique yet natural attribute that other beings apparently do not exhibit, namely, free will.

I offer eight reasons why a belief in free will makes very good sense. Four of these explain why there can be initiative—that is, why nature does not preclude it. But these do not yet demonstrate that initiative exists. That will be shown by the other four reasons, which will establish that initiative actually exists.

Nature versus Initiative

First, one of the major objections to initiative is that nature is governed by a set of laws, mainly the laws of physics. Everything is controlled by these laws, and we human beings are basically more complicated versions of material substances; therefore, whatever governs any other material substance in the universe must also govern human life. Basically, we are subject to the same kind of causation to which everything else is. Since nothing else exhibits initiative but everything conforms to causal laws, so must we.[24] Social science is merely looking into the particulars of those causes, but we all know that we are subject to them in any case. The only difference is that we are complicated things.

In response I point óut that nature exhibits innumerable different domains, distinct not only in their complexity but also in the kinds of beings they include. So it is not possible to rule out ahead of time that there might be something in nature that exhibits agent causation. This is the phenomenon whereby a thing causes some of its own behavior. So there might be in nature a form of existence that exhibits initiative. Whether there is or not is something to be discovered, not ruled out by a metaphysical conception of cause that restricts everything and thus every kind of cause to being a variation on just one kind of thing and cause. Thus, taking account of what nature is composed of does not at all rule out initiative.

Knowledge and Initiative

Another reason why some think that initiative is not possible is that the dominant mode of studying, inspecting, or examining nature is what we call "empiricism." In other words, many believe that the only way we know about nature is to observe it with our various sensory organs. But since the sensory organs do not give us direct evidence of

---

24. "The human mind remains extraordinarily difficult to understand, but so is the weather. . . . I see nothing about the human mind any more than about the weather that stands out as beyond the hope of understanding as a consequence of impersonal laws acting over billions of years." Steven Weinberg, "A Designer Universe?" *New York Review of Books* 46, no. 16 (October 21, 1999): 46. For a very informative and productive discussion of this, see Edward Pols, *Mind Regained* (Ithaca, N.Y.: Cornell University Press, 1998).

such a thing as free will, there really is no such thing. Since no observable evidence for initiative exists, initiative does not exist.

But the doctrine that empiricism captures all forms of knowing is wrong. We know many things not simply through observation but through a combination of observation, inferences, and theory construction. (Consider: Even the purported knowledge that empiricism is our form of knowledge could not be "known" empirically!)

For one, many features of the universe, including criminal guilt, are usually detected without eyewitnesses but by way of theories that serve the purpose of best explaining what we do have before us to observe. This is true even in the natural sciences. Many of the phenomena or facts in biology, astrophysics, subatomic physics, botany, and chemistry—not to mention psychology—consist not of what we see or detect by observation but what is inferred by way of a theory and the concepts in terms of which we understand the world. And the theory that explains things best, most completely and most consistently, is the best answer to the question as to what is going on. If it is a theory that solves all current problems and does so without inconsistencies, it is true.[25]

Initiative may well turn out to be in this category. In other words, the capacity to initiate conduct is not directly observed but constitutes a fact that best explains some crucial aspects of human life. This includes, for example, the many mistakes that human beings make in contrast to the few mistakes that other animals make. We also notice that human beings do all kinds of odd things that cannot be accounted for in terms of mechanical causation, the type associated with physics. We can examine a person's background and find that some people with bad childhoods turn out to be decent, whereas others turn out to be criminals. The wide variety of cultural and ethnic differences, as well as individuality itself, could not be accounted for without this

---

25. "True" does not mean "never in need of any further revision, updating, modification," as, unfortunately, many believe.

capacity. Initiative explains all this, makes sense of it, renders it intelligible.

For now all we need to consider is that this may well be so, and if empiricism and mechanism do not allow for it, so much the worse for them. One can know something because it explains other things better than any alternative, and that is not itself strict empirical knowledge. This gives rise to the strong possibility of agent causation or initiative. In other words, once empiricism is demoted as the reigning conception of human knowing, the possibility that we could know that free will or initiative exists is not precluded.

Is Initiative Peculiar?

Another matter that very often counts against initiative is that the rest of living nature does not exhibit it. Dogs, cats, lizards, fish, and frogs, have no free will, and therefore it appears arbitrary to impute it to human beings. Why should we be free to do things when the rest of nature lacks any such capacity? It would be an impossible aberration.

The answer here is similar to that given earlier. To wit, there is enough variety in nature—some things swim, some fly, some just lie there, some breathe, some grow, whereas others do not. So there is sufficient evidence of plurality of types and kinds of things in nature. Discovering that something has free will could be yet another addition to all the varieties of nature.

Let us now consider—again, for now only in a sketchy fashion—whether initiative actually does exist. Following are four arguments in support of an affirmative answer. Each separately might not clinch the case for free will, but jointly they offer a case that is compelling.

Determinism's Dilemma

There is an argument against determinism to the effect that, if we are fully determined in what we think, believe, and do, then of course the belief that determinism is true is also a result of this determinism. So the same must hold for the belief that determinism is false. You have to believe what you do because it is determined.

There is no way to take an independent stance and consider the arguments unprejudiced because of all the various forces making us assimilate the evidence in the world just the way we do. One either turns out to be a determinist or not, and in neither case can we appraise the issue objectively, because we are predetermined to have a view on the matter one way or the other.

But then, paradoxically, we will never be able to resolve this debate, since there is no way of obtaining an objective assessment. Indeed, the very idea of scientific or judicial objectivity, as well as of ever reaching philosophical truth, has to do with being free. Thus, if we are engaged in this enterprise of learning about truth and distinguishing it from falsehood, we are committed to the idea that human beings have some measure of mental freedom.

Determinism's Imperative

There is another dilemma of determinism. The determinist wants us to believe in determinism. In fact, he or she believes we ought to be determinists rather than believing in this myth called "initiative." But, as the saying goes in philosophy, "ought" implies "can." That is, if one ought to believe in or do something, this implies that one has a choice in the matter; it implies that we can make a choice as to whether determinism or initiative is a better doctrine. That, then, presupposes that we are free. In other words, even arguing for determinism assumes that we are not determined to believe in free will, but that it is a matter of our making certain choices about arguments, evidence, and thinking itself.[26]

26. One may argue that all the determinist is saying is that it would be better to

Some have addressed this point by claiming that all we do when we argue for or against something is to act as causal forces upon others, as instruments to impel their minds to change. We are not assuming they can do anything on their own initiative; quite the contrary. We are very much set on forcing a change in them.

This objection suggests that when we are discussing controversial matters, we are engaging in manipulation, plain and simple. We are not trying to convince anyone—that is, in any case, a misguided notion, fitting within the framework of free will but not of determinism. We are ourselves simply moved to move others, ad infinitum.

We will have to consider eventually whether this makes adequate sense of human discourse, dialogue, communication. At first inspection it certainly does not seem to. What I am doing is not, ordinarily understood, just moving my fingers over the keyboard of my computer, forced to type away as I do, with no place for my own initiative. I seem clearly to have chosen to embark upon the writing of this work, and each time I return to the project, I make the effort, take the initiative to do so. And the determinist is telling me that I am off base, wrong, and should think differently from how I have convinced myself to think about the matter—namely, that I govern my own actions and am not compelled by factors apart from my own initiative to take them.

Witnessing Our Freedom

In many contexts of our lives introspective knowledge is taken very seriously. When a doctor asks where our pain is located, we answer that it is in the knee. The doctor does not then inform us that

---

believe in determinism than not to—not that one ought to believe in it.

Yet the "ought" is implicit in our addressing ourselves to the idea, since that only makes sense if there is the expectation that we may change our minds. Some of this is discussed in Joseph Boyle, Germain Gabriel Grisez, and Olaf Tollefsen, *Free Choice* (Notre Dame, Ind.: University of Notre Dame Press, 1976). See also Jordan, "Determinism's Dilemma."

no one can know this since there is no public evidence at hand. The doctor does not protest, but rather sets about obtaining verifiable, direct evidence of the pain. In fact, the evidence given by the person is the best possible.

Witnesses at trials give evidence as they report about what they have seen, which rests, in part, on a species of introspection, namely, memory: "I recall that this indeed is what I have seen or heard." Even in the various natural sciences, people report on the data they have gathered or readings they have seen on gauges or instruments. Thus they are depending on introspective evidence.

Introspection is, thus, one source of evidence that we take as reasonably reliable. So what should we make of the fact that a lot of people do say things like, "Damn it, I didn't make the right choice," or "I neglected to do something." They report to us that they have made various choices and decisions, that they intended this or that but not another thing. "I meant to turn back there but wasn't paying attention." And people often blame themselves for not having done something; thus they report that they are taking responsibility for what they have or have not done. "I ought to have stopped smoking long ago" or "I raised my voice against him and I shouldn't have done it." And in even more mundane ways we see ourselves as free, as when we fail to heed a doctor's advice to favor a foot or not to make use of a limb for a while. And even less overtly, when we stop chewing on one side of our mouth because we need to guard one of our teeth. The same occurs when we speak and use the wrong word or when we write and fail to express ourselves properly, misspell words, or deploy bad grammar.

If we fail in such tasks, we blame ourselves, indicating that we think we could have done as we should have. Misspeaking oneself when talking with a sensitive relative or colleague and feeling regret or handling some delicate matter discreetly and feeling some pride testify to our conviction that we have control over such matters, even though they result not from deliberation but from simple intention. (At this point we could take a longish detour to consider the subtle differences between will, intention, deliberation, wanting, desiring, and so forth, but I shall leave that aside for now.)

In short, there is considerable evidence, from our own conduct and from that of others around us, of the existence of free choice. Sometimes one's exercise of choice is explicitly reported, sometimes it is implied in one's regrets and self-criticism or sense of achievement.

Initiative and Science

There is also evidence of the fact that we have the capacity for self-monitoring. The human brain is structured so as to allow us to govern ourselves. We can inspect our lives, we can detect where we are going, and we can, therefore, change course. Because of the brain's structure, we can monitor ourselves, and as a result we can decide whether to continue in a certain pattern or to change that pattern and go in a different direction. That is the sort of initiative that is demonstrable. At least some scientists, such as the late Roger W. Sperry,[27] maintain that there is evidence for initiative in this sense. This view depends on a number of points I have already mentioned. It assumes that there can be different kinds of causes in nature, so that the functioning of the brain would be a kind of self-causation, or, rather, initiation. As Sperry notes:

> There exists within the cranium a whole world of diverse causal forces, as in no other cubic half-foot of universe that we know . . . [and] if one keeps climbing upward in the chain of command within the brain, one finds at the very top those overall organizational forces

27. Roger W. Sperry, *Science and Moral Priority* (New York: Columbia University Press, 1983) and his numerous technical papers in such journals as *Perspectives in Biology and Medicine*.

and dynamic properties of the large patterns the overall cerebral
excitation that are correlated with mental states or psychic activity.

So, accordingly,

> [T]he kind of determinism proposed is not that of the atomic, molec-
> ular, or cellular level, but rather the kind that prevails at the level of
> cerebral mentation, involving the interplay of ideas, reasoning pro-
> cesses, judgments, emotion, insight, and so forth.[28]

By means of the brain as a system we are able to cause some aspects
of our organism's behavior. This in turn depends on the possibility of
there being various kinds of causation, including agent or initial causation.

Precisely the sort of thing Sperry thinks possible is evident in our
lives. We make plans and revise them. We explore alternatives and
decide to follow one of them. We change a course of conduct we have
embarked upon or continue with it. In other words, there is a locus of
individual self-responsibility that is evident in the way in which we
look upon ourselves and the way in which we in fact behave.

IS IT TRUE THAT WE HAVE INITIATIVE?

Finally, when we put all of this together, we get a more sensible
understanding of the complexities of human life. We get a better understanding, for example, of why social engineering and government
regulation and regimentation do not work, why there are so many
individual and cultural differences, why people can be wrong, why
they can disagree with each other, and so forth. It is because people
are free to do so, because they are not fixed in some pattern as are
cats, dogs, orangutans, and birds.

Most of the behavior of these creatures can be predicted. So, too,

---

28. Sperry, *Science and Moral Priority*, 33–34, 39.

can some human behavior, but mainly because people often have their minds made up, and from that it is possible to estimate what they are going to do. But even then we do not get a certain prediction. Very often people change their minds and surprise us. And if we go to different cultures, they will surprise us even more. This complexity, diversity, and individuation of human beings is best explained by the fact that human beings are free rather than determined.

WE HAVE GOOD REASON
TO TRUST INITIATIVE

So these several reasons provide a compressed argumentative collage in support of the free-will position. In this book I expand on each element of the collage. Assuming, for now, that such a collage is available to us, would it be sufficient to show that we do, indeed, have free will, that we are capable of exerting initiative?

Which is the best of the various competing theories? Are human beings behaving solely in mechanistic or otherwise unalterable response to forces impinging on them? Or do they have the capacity to take charge of their lives, often neglecting to do so properly or effectively, making stupid choices, and so forth? Which supposition best explains the human world and its complexities, and which has more convincing arguments to back it up?

The idea that we have free will and can take the initiative makes much better sense than its converse. Even our brief overview suggests that much. Human beings remake the world, again for better or worse, without having to do so—although naturally within the limits of what is possible in their circumstances.

Given our capacity for initiating some of our own conduct, it seems, furthermore, highly unlikely that any formula or system is going to predictably manage the future of human affairs, in the way some of the social sciences hope for. Social engineering is thus not a genuine prospect for solving human problems—only education and individual initiative can do that. This, to be sure, is in need of further demonstration. Yet we have already seen some convincing points that support the idea. And we can also appreciate the practical implications that the existence of human initiative, free will, has for human social and political life—persons ought to be treated as self-directed and not as passive, malleable, inert subjects to be regimented in their lives.

PROBLEMS WITH THE "AS IF" THESIS

There are those, of course, who hold that there is room both for causal determinism and for praise and blame. They claim that even if there were no such thing as initiative, treating people as if they were free agents produces positive results (i.e., results that we ourselves— all or most of us—are causally destined to deem as positive). The idea is that praising and blaming can produce consequences even if, strictly speaking, individuals cannot be blamed or praised for acting as they do since they have no capacity to determine their own conduct.

Yet taking this tack capitalizes on a conceptual difference between being convinced about something and being fooled into believing it, a distinction that assumes initiative. Those who are fooled are deemed, generally, to have the capacity to watch out against that eventuality—unless, of course, they were made to be fooled. Furthermore, underlying this thesis we still find several questions that raise the issue of genuine initiative. Also, knowing the meaning of the praise or blame would be necessary in order to achieve the desired consequence—a person would need to believe that he or she is capable of making a difference in his or her conduct.

For example, should those who are onto the illusion keep people in the dark about their belief in free will? Are we free or determined to make that decision? Is it right to fool people about such matters? If not, is it up to us to desist?

Also, if the free will matter is a case of *as if*, what if most people discover it? Surely, if philosophers and psychologists can learn that it is merely a matter of treating us as if we had initiative, so can others, in which case there is no point in continuing the subterfuge.

Finally, in fact, praise and blame do not make sense, have no coherent point, if there is no factual basis for them. When we praise or blame dogs or horses, at most we are engaging in a kind of reinforcement or encouragement, something that makes them feel good and induces repetition. This is not genuine praise or blame, which aims not simply at changing behavior but at doing so by means of inducing guilt or pride, neither of which is possible or developed sufficiently at the animal level.

To repeat, in order to play the *as if* game, there must be some possibility of genuine praise or blame. Barring that, they cannot be effective at inducing bona fide pride or guilt. The language of ethics would be discovered to be no different from that of demonology or witchcraft, resting on nothing but error or myth.

LAW, PUBLIC POLICY, AND INITIATIVE

I now briefly touch on the subject of why free will is a proper subject matter to raise in connection with our understanding of ethics, law, and public policies.

To start with, let us return briefly to Kant's contribution to this issue with his philosophical motto, "ought implies can." In other words, we cannot have the responsibility to do or abstain from doing an action if the action is not something we can initiate. This initiation may be very well hidden when the action actually occurs, so that we may simply attribute its origin to character or some early commitment or choice. But in that case, we would have to be able to make sense of the idea that the character traits or skills that prompted the action were learned and cultivated by the individual who has them or that the commitments and choices we make are our own doing and not something we were compelled to do.[29]

Let us again recall the insight expressed in Kant's motto—one evidenced, also, in Aristotle's observation that "the virtues are modes of choice or involve choice" and that "it is in our power to be virtuous or vicious."[30] We can see from it that any effort to credit or discredit persons for good or bad behavior without initiative, including the support of good or bad public policies, institutions, and so forth, would amount to meaningless gestures. It is akin to invoking the concept of a ghost without admitting to a spiritual realm of reality. Without the latter, ghosts are impossible.

Take an intellectual climate in which initiative is rejected, as it clearly is when misconduct is routinely attributed to addiction or other afflictions. There the idea that someone has the power to initiate a change in his conduct (if only in whether and how he or she thinks

---

29. Very complex traits and skills emerge in people as a result of sustained choice or commitment, including highly developed musical or athletic techniques, and virtues such as fidelity, prudence, and generosity. For more on this idea, see Tibor R. Machan, *Generosity: Virtue in Civil Society* (Washington, D.C.: Cato Institute, 1998).

30. Aristotle, *Nicomachean Ethics* 2.5.1106a2, 1113b13. It is interesting that Kekes, in *Facing Evil*, classifies his own views as akin to those of Aristotle, in virtue of their being on the side of character as distinct from (Kantian) choice moralities. Yet Aristotle connects moral virtue with choice and ties being vicious and virtuous to our power to be one or the other. These features of Aristotle's ethics—or rather metaethics—appear to place Aristotle's version of character morality within the class of choice moralities.

Indeed, it is arguable that Kekes's "ethics" is only a theory of value. It has little to say about morality as such. The latter is a special category of value, namely, the realization or loss of which the agent can bring about on his or her own (within, of course, the requisite setting in the world). When Kekes explains morality, he in fact describes only a theory of values based on the enhancement of human life. Yet many factors enhance or damage human life, some of them brought about by persons, some of them not, so it is important for the cogency of any bona fide morality that personal initiative be explained. It also seems that by Kekes's account many higher life forms participate in the moral life.

about the issues involved) makes no sense. This is just what we witness when someone is being urged to stop smoking and answers, "Well, I just can't stop." Even when genetic predisposition is involved, there is the alternative of our having or lacking a measure of control over it.[31]

If all evaluations of human behavior could be met with, "Well, I just cannot do otherwise," this surely would have an impact on our self-understanding and on whether we can make the effort needed to improve our lives. Moral advice, exhortation, criticism, praise, reward, and the like would be robbed of their meaning, just as the idea that someone is a witch or inhabited by demons is largely looked upon as meaningless in a climate that deems magic impossible.

Accordingly, there seems to be a drastic gap between the idea of human nature that is afoot these days and is tacitly accepted by many social scientists, philosophers, and other professional thinkers and researchers and the persistent moralizing that goes on in our culture, including in scholarly journals. Perhaps this is of no concern to some people, but there is at least one moral reason to think of it as a serious issue—one that might even be construed as a matter of applied ethics, namely, the ethics of philosophical scholarship. That reason is integrity.

Integrity means having the various facets of one's ideas, values, and policies in life, including one's professional pronouncements, placed in some sort of a consistent, coherent—integrated—framework. If, in fact, one can live with both a deterministic conception of human action and extensive moralizing, integrity would not be a necessary part of human life and certainly not of the life of a philosopher

---

31. Even Richard Dawkins, in his renowned book *The Selfish Gene* (London: Oxford University Press, 1989), proclaims that we can "rebel" against our genes and that, although they are statistically a very strong influence, they do not determine what we do (pp. 331–32).

who dabbles in these issues. But then this could also have an impact on how we should view politicians and others whose lack of integrity is so often the topic of applied ethics discussions.[32]

If, however, we affirm the reality of initiative, we might also have to adjust some of our moral claims. In business ethics, for example, the doctrine of consumer sovereignty is commonly challenged on grounds advanced by John Kenneth Galbraith, namely, that consumers are easily manipulated by advertisements to purchase goods and services they do not actually need or want.[33] If, however, some version of initiative is construed as necessarily presupposed by business ethics as such, it may well require construing consumer sovereignty as something more reasonable than Galbraith claims. Other examples of issues that may be influenced by a thorough discussion of the free-will issue involve such often-dismissed notions as "caveat emptor" ("let the buyer beware") or "unconscionable contract" and certain ways of understanding surrogate mothering or sexual exploitation or domination. In the area of sexual harassment, molestation, and assault problems, the idea is often advanced that some people are incapable of resisting their urges to make advances toward—even at times to rape—others who appear very attractive or provocative to them. Here, too, the free-will stance would, if sound, discredit this way of understanding and open the way to assigning responsibility to individuals who sexually harass, molest, or rape, as well as to those who misman-

32. To pick just one topic, what is "lack of fairness" if not a lack of integrity as applied in a certain domain of one's conduct?

33. John Kenneth Galbraith, "The Dependence Effect," reprinted in numerous business ethics texts and collections, from his work *The Affluent Society*. See, for example, Thomas L. Beauchamp and Norman E. Bowie, *Ethical Theory and Business* (Englewood Cliffs, N.J.: Prentice-Hall, 1983). See a discussion of this issue in Douglas J. Den Uyl's essay on advertising in Tibor R. Machan, ed., *Commerce and Morality* (Totowa, N.J.: Rowman and Littlefield, 1988). See also F. A. Hayek's essay, "The Non-sequitur of 'The Dependence Effect,'" in a few business ethics collections, for example, Beauchamp and Bowie.

age their lives by way of procrastination, intemperance, immoderation, and other minor vices. That is to say, with initiative or causal power a real element of human action, the person who acts would stand in for an ultimate explanation of his or her behavior.[34]

Finally, there are those who attribute racist, sexist, and other kinds of unjust sentiments entirely to their upbringing, claiming that given how or where they were brought up, it is impossible for them to feel and act differently from the way they do. They should not be made to pay for something they cannot help—it is, after all, an unavoidable fact that they are the way they are and could do nothing about it.

It seems to me that these ways of looking at misconduct by human beings are undermined by the free-will thesis, provided it is sound. If it is not sound, these ways of thinking would be quite feasible and very possibly solid, although, as I argue shortly, it is questionable whether we could know this.

In any case, without a direct examination of the connection between ethics and the initiative issue, we should be candid in admitting that ethics is fundamentally bogus and that the questions of morality, politics, and public policy are without substance. This is indeed what some have argued who have concluded that no human initiative is possible and that everything happens because it has to happen.

As to whether some room could be left for ethics, morality, and other normative concerns about human conduct, I do not believe that there could be without free will or initiative. Suppose that what we do has to be done—that no genuine alternative to what we actually do exists at the time we do it (or existed at an earlier time when the course of action was set into motion). Then talk about people being responsible for what they do, about how they ought to have done something other than what they did do, and the like must be dismissed as non-

---

34. For a full discussion of this matter, see Edward Pols, *The Acts of Our Being* (Amherst, Mass.: University of Massachusetts Press, 1982).

sense, as, to use the late B. F. Skinner's language, "prescientific" mutterings. Ethics and other normative fields should be cast into the intellectual trash bin, along with astrology, witchcraft, and phrenology.

Oddly, however, often the same thinkers and commentators who would deprive some people of the capacity to choose are, nevertheless, willing to ascribe this capacity to others, especially to corporations. Thus tobacco—and, more recently, some fattening food and drink—is deemed to be an irresistible consumer product. So consumers are deemed incapable of stopping its use even when they have been fully apprised of the dangers of the practice. In turn, the companies—which means various other people—marketing the product are deemed fully liable for the damage they are said to have caused to smokers. The suggestion seems to be that different classes of people possess different capacities for choosing what they do. Perhaps the wealthy are free to choose, and only those lacking sufficient wealth are determined to behave as circumstances make them.

Yet this could not be a serious option. As noted already, company officials who promote cigarette smoking could have been caused to behave as they do by their upbringing and professional training. Arguably, those trained to do business at the Harvard Graduate School of Business could have been inculcated with certain traits, and they are no more able to resist the behavior these traits impel than consumers are able to resist their addiction. No one, then, is responsible for the bad health that results from both the ensuing vigorous marketing and repeated consumption.

If, however, ordinary human beings possess the capacity to cause some of their significant behavior—for example, whether they will market or smoke cigarettes—they would have to shoulder the consequences that arise from this practice. Marketers would be responsible for the proliferation of attention being paid to the availability of cigarettes and smokers for the health problems their decision to smoke (and refusal to quit) causes.[35]

It is clear, then, that whether or not human beings have free will or the capacity to exercise initiative in their lives—to cause some things to happen on their own accord—can have serious legal and public policy consequences.

35. Of course, exceptions could be found, as well. Some may have congenital afflictions or incapacities, so they might not have the power to resist—as some people are allergic to peanuts or penicillin. Charges of liability would have to be adjusted accordingly.

CHAPTER ONE

Initiative,
Opposed and Defended

NATURE'S LAWS VERSUS INITIATIVE

Elementary Scientism

The most frequent objection to free will is that the laws of nature, those that the various hard or natural sciences identify, make it impossible. Such laws are universal. They amount to regularities involving events that cause other events in an everlasting chain throughout the natural world. There is, then, no room for human initiative in nature since all human behaviors (or actions or conduct) are caused by events that preceded and produced them.

The most explicit and accessible statement of this view was advanced by the late B. F. Skinner of Harvard University, one of the giants of behaviorist psychology. Others have made the point less prominently but no less insistently. Nothing but efficient causation exists in nature, whereby events link to other events constituting the infinite causal chain that is the ongoing process of reality.

Paul and Patricia Churchland are two philosophers who have defended the view that the human mind ought to be understood on the model of sophisticated machines or computers. They have said also that they did not wish to bother themselves with "this, that, or the

other preconceived notion of human freedom, [but] recommend, that
we let scientific investigation teach us which way and to what degree
human creatures are 'free.'"[1]

Just why it must be left to scientific investigation to decide on this
issue can be appreciated when it is also understood that for many
people it is only the efficient causal powers that can be detected via
observation that carry any credibility. Such causal power is what we
see when a cue ball strikes another on a pool table.

Yet, as we shall see, reliance on such detection is misplaced,
because observation always operates in conjunction with inference
and other conceptual processes. If these processes "detect" different
sorts of causal powers from the mechanical, efficient type, those too
must be given credence.[2]

Evolution and Free Will

Often when even the most intelligent people speak about evolution, they tend to assume that such a process must be deterministic or
fatalistic. It must explain everything in human life, judging by the
plethora of books and essays produced by evolutionary biologists. It
can explain altruism, cooperation, cultural variety, morality, or the
emotion of hatred, to pick just a few examples from the current litera-

---

1. Paul M. and Patricia S. Churchland, *On The Contrary* (Boston, Mass.: MIT
Press, 1998), p. 77. The most recent candidates for determining complex human
behavior are memes—which Robert Aunger calls "not the [physical] network of
neurons [but] a property of the network: its readiness-to-fire"—so identified by Richard Dawkins in his *The Selfish Gene* (London: Oxford University Press, 1976). Much
of what we do is determined by genes but "the crucial memetic postulate is that a
second replicator—memes—leapt into the power gap." Robert Aunger, "Culture
Vultures," *The Sciences*, September/October 1999, p. 40.

2. Arguably, scientific investigation can amount to something other than strictly
empirical observation. It could also involve the kind of explorations done by careful
philosophers. After all, mathematics is a science that is carried out almost entirely
independently of observations.

ture and from discussion groups on the Internet. The underlying assumption in most such treatments is that whatever happened had to have happened, that whatever happens must happen, and whatever did not could not have.

In other words, determinism and evolution often go hand in hand. For some, as I have already noted, the only place where freedom may have room is in the realm of the mysterious, where morality arises. Even Charles Darwin appears to have suggested something along these lines:

> I fully subscribe to the judgment of those writers who maintain that of all the differences between man and the lower animals, the moral sense or conscience is by far the most important. This sense, as Mackintosh remarks, "has a rightful supremacy over every other principle of human action"; it is summed up in that short but imperious word ought, so full of high significance. It is the most noble of all the attributes of man, leading him without a moment's hesitation to risk his life for that of a fellow creature; or after due deliberation, impelled simply by the deep feeling of right or duty, to sacrifice it in some great cause. Immanuel Kant exclaims, "Duty! Wondrous thought, that workest neither by fond insinuation, flattery, nor by any threat, but merely by holding up thy naked law in the soul, and so extorting for thyself always reverence, if not always obedience; before whom all appetites are dumb, however secretly they rebel; whence thy original?"
> The following proposition seems to me in a high degree probable— namely, that any animal whatever, endowed with well-marked social instincts, the parental and filial affections being here included, would inevitably acquire a moral sense or conscience, as soon as its intellectual powers had become as well, or nearly as well developed, as in man. For, firstly, the social instincts lead an animal to take pleasure in the society of its fellows, to feel a certain amount of sympathy with them, and to perform various services for them. The services may be of a definite and evidently instinctive nature; or there may be only a wish and readiness, as with most of the higher social animals, to aid their fellows in certain general ways. But these feelings and services

are by no means extended to all the individuals of the same species, only to those of the same association. Secondly, as soon as the mental faculties had become highly developed, images of all past actions and motives would be incessantly passing through the brain of each individual: and that feeling of dissatisfaction, or even misery, which invariably results, as we shall hereafter see, from any unsatisfied instinct, would arise, as often as it was perceived that the enduring and always present social instinct had yielded to some other instinct, at the time stronger, but neither enduring in its nature, nor leaving behind it a very vivid impression. It is clear that many instinctive desires, such as that of hunger, are in their nature of short duration and, after being satisfied, are not readily or vividly recalled. Thirdly, after the power of language had been acquired, and the wishes of the community could be expressed, the common opinion about how each member ought to act for the public good would naturally become, in a paramount degree, the guide to action. But it should be borne in mind that however great weight we may attribute to public opinion, our regard for the approbation and disapprobation of our fellows depends on sympathy, which, as we shall see, forms an essential part of the social instinct, and is indeed its foundation-stone. Lastly, habit in the individual would ultimately play a very important part in guiding the conduct of each member; for the social instinct, together with sympathy, is, like any other instinct, greatly strengthened by habit, and so consequently would be obedience to the wishes and judgment of the community.[3]

As eloquent and insightful as this account is, it leaves little room for bona fide free will, since Darwin, like David Hume and Adam Smith, proposes that an innate propensity or sentiment exists in all of us to act sympathetically, benevolently, and kindly toward others. The "ought" is at most a superior inclination or built-in imperative, very much a part of the system of biological laws that produces all other aspects of the living world.

So even though some effort is made by Darwin and many of his

3. Charles Darwin, *Descent of Man* (Buffalo, N.Y.: Prometheus Books, 1997).

followers—for example, Edward O. Wilson—to leave room for morality, it is not for the morality that presupposes free choice ("ought" implies "can"). The basic idea remains that there is an ineluctable process throughout the living world that drives the development of all living things, including all the commendable behavior higher animals engage in. Richard Dawkins's *The Selfish Gene* is perhaps the most developed statement of this view, to the effect that the evolutionary process in which genetic development occurs drives everything we do and that there can be no alternative but to do what genes make us do. Yet, as I pointed out in the introduction, even Dawkins says that we have control over our actions and can resist the pressure of our genes, although he gives no clear reason for this exception other than to say that consciousness and self-awareness make it possible. Steven Pinker's *How the Mind Works* also lays out such a view, although with some caveats of a Kantian kind that we have already noted. Another is Daniel Dennett's *Darwin's Dangerous Idea.*[4]

To these and others we may offer the following observations from Kennan Malik:

> Implicitly, evolutionary psychologists understand that the human mind cannot be understood in simple Darwinian terms because humans often act contrary to Darwinian principles. Thus, in his book *Evolution in Mind*, the psychologist Henry Plotkin opens his discussion on human culture by claiming that "there is not much intellec-

---

4. For a powerful criticism of evolutionary psychology, which is based on if not identical to the neo-Darwinism we found in Wilson, Dennett, and others, see Kennan Malik, "The Darwinian Fallacy," *Prospect* 35 (December 1998): 24–30. This criticism is unrelated to what has recently emerged from religious and theological circles; it is one that is directed not so much against evolutionary theory as such but against the naturalism that underlies it, often mistakenly dubbed "materialism." Materialism presupposes that nature is composed of something we call "matter," even though no such thing exists. Naturalism, in contrast, assumes nothing about what kinds of beings there are in nature, only that whatever they are, they conform to the most basic laws of nature—for example, the law of identity and noncontradiction—and are not subject to magical or miraculous forces.

tual risk . . . in making the assumption that human culture is the product of human evolution." A few pages later, though, he is forced to admit to a problem with this view. If "culture is the direct product of evolution," how is it possible, he asks, for culture to create forms that can "adversely affect our biological fitness?" How can we understand celibacy or the risking of life and limb in wars? "The only explanation," Plotkin believes, "is that culture entails causal mechanisms that are somehow decoupled . . . from the causal mechanisms of our biological evolution." Dawkins similarly writes in *The Selfish Gene* that while "we are built as gene machines . . . we have the power to turn against our creators." Steven Pinker has put this point most boldly of all. "By Darwinian standards," he writes, "I am a horrible mistake." Why? Because he has chosen to remain childless. "I am happy to be that way," he adds, "and if my genes don't like it they can go and jump in the lake."[5]

Evolved Initiative

Not all evolutionary theorists champion determinism. Theodosius Dobzhansky has argued for what the title of one of his works calls *The Biological Basis of Human Freedom*.[6] More recently, Steven Rose has argued a similar thesis in his *Lifelines: Biology beyond Determinism*.[7]

There is no justification for the claim that an evolutionary process governing the emergence and processes of human existence must contradict free will. Consider that the evolutionary process has produced beings that can swim, fly, or crawl, all highly varied forms of life, involving great varieties of processes. Why, then, could it not produce, also, something that must generate its own survival and thriving? Why couldn't the evolutionary process produce a thing that possesses free

5. Malik, "Darwinian Fallacy," p. 29.

6. Theodosius Dobzhansky, *The Biological Basis of Human Freedom* (New York: Columbia University Press, 1956).

7. Steven Rose, *Lifelines: Biology beyond Determinism* (London: Oxford University Press, 1998).

will? No reason precludes this—that is, provided free will is understood in a nonmysterious fashion and provided we do not quite unsci-
entifically build into evolution the process of mechanical causation.

What if having free will means no more than that whoever has it
can start to do some important things without having to be made to do
them? What if it is the power of initiative, of creative or original action,
such as thinking, that has evolved with human life?

There is nothing unnatural about human initiative unless we build
into our idea of nature something absolutely or fully fatalistic and
deterministic, or unless we accept the view that all causation must be
of one sort. There is, in both of these assumptions, an implicit substance metaphysics that is not argued for by evolutionary theorists.
Accordingly, only those kinds of beings can exist in nature that take
part in a causal process of events leading to other events, a never-
ending chain that accommodates the alleged fact that things are all
the same and can only participate in one kind of causal interaction.

This, however, is presumptuous and begs the question of what
kinds of beings there can be in nature. As I have noted before, it is
unscientific to come at the issue of human agency with prejudice,
assuming that nature cannot manifest such agency. If evolution is a
general process of the living world, what it can give rise to must
equally be left to be discovered, not imposed a priori.

Assuming that human initiative exists, it would give rise to unex-
pected creativity, to original ideas, and, thus, to developments in human affairs. For example, the emergence of cloning or the postpone-
ment of parenthood via saving frozen embryos for later full
development, could both amount to such creativity. Such creativity
seems to be presupposed in our understanding of the great variety that
is manifest in human living. Different cultures, religions, sports, styles
of art or clothing, technology, political concepts, and so forth, all suggest that unlike other animals, the fate of the human species is not
preordained but produced by exceedingly creative human initiative.

Apart from free will, there is another thing that has occupied the minds of many thinkers since Charles Darwin put evolutionary biology on the agenda of human thought. This is morality. Where does it stand within the context of evolution?

The short of this is that morality, too, could, and probably does, fit well within the course of nature's development. With the kind of life that human beings live, wherein they need to make various original moves or start to act on their own initiative, the question arises as to what they ought to do. They need to have, as a matter of their essential nature, a standard by which to distinguish right from wrong conduct. This is one way they differ from nonhuman animals that possess instincts or innate drives that provide answers without their having to choose to discover them. For nonhuman animals, the question simply does not and cannot arise.

CAN WE KNOW OF INITIATIVE?

Empiricist Prejudices

Among those who do not rest their view of the world on faith, the preferred conception of knowing is empiricist. "I am from Missouri, show me," tends to be their motto. Social scientists, even more than those in the natural sciences, have held out this idea—that sheer observation is the sole or primary requirement for coming to know things—as the standard to be met to defend a knowledge claim.

Yet in many natural sciences knowing often is accomplished by means of elaborate inferences and what is called inference to the best explanation, akin to what happens in crime detection. Facts that are evident need to be accounted for; hypotheses are advanced, and the one that holds up best—is most powerful, consistent, complete, and so forth—ends up as the right answer, what one can justifiably claim to know.

Still, in the social sciences the empiricist model has reigned throughout the contemporary era. In consequence, a fact of social life that isn't ascertainable by looking and measuring what one sees or senses by some other means is often discounted. Human initiative or free will is a case in point.

No one can observe someone's initiative through the senses. When one begins to do something, that origination or initial action is not observed directly. Based on observation alone, no one could tell whether it is what those who argue for it claim.

Therefore, one may maintain that human beings do things on their own initiative, but this cannot be proven by pointing at some empirically observable data; thus the claim is discounted. Even when no other explanation has been shown to be sound, it is often held that there must be some event that causes people to do what they did. (This is often assumed to be a requirement of science itself, although actually it is not. Rather, the assumption comes from a metaphysical framework that demands determinism from all the sciences.[8]) Referring to a person's initiative thus seems to be insupportable as an answer to why he or she did something.

There are many problems with empiricism, and in epistemology, or the theory of knowledge, it is not upheld with great confidence. First, the claim that we know by way of observation alone is not itself supportable by way of observation alone. It is a theory, an explanation of how we know, not some data we can point at. And such theories never rest solely on observation but require making conceptual connections and inferences that, if empiricism were correct, would be ill grounded. Second, most so-called observations are not simply such. Instead, they are theory-laden accounts of something. Even when we see a table in the living room, we do not simply record sensations but combine what we observe with our understanding of what a table is. That is one reason that so-called eyewitness testimony is often so varied from one to another eyewitness—the witness casts the observation in a certain light, based on what he or she believes or knows

8. Tom Sorell, *Scientism* (London: Routledge, 1991).

apart from the observation itself. (Popular cases of such a problem occur when people claim to have seen the face of someone in the clouds. In fact, the face is not there but is the product of putting together what is there, clouds of a certain shape, with some other shape one remembers and associates with some person.)

Unfortunately, the fact that what we believe exists and even know is not the result of observation alone has often suggested something equally implausible, namely, that we ourselves have constructed the thing and that no such thing really does exist. But there is no reason to hold this view. A more plausible alternative is to realize that we learn certain rules of understanding the world from the initial understanding that we have gained about simple things in the world. We learn that things persist over time, remain intact, have a history, are composed of matter we can get at by breaking it up, and so forth. The integrity of things we encounter—and the fact that no such integrity would be possible if there were no laws of nature that govern how things are and behave—establishes by inference the ubiquity of integrity. So we do not bother to always break them into their small parts to make sure we have things right.

We see a rabbit, but we do not check through our entire array of animal taxonomy to make sure each time that rabbits are indeed a distinct species of animal. So we take it that the mere exposure to what can be seen of rabbits suffices to know that it is indeed a rabbit out there that we see.

Detecting the various things in the world, then, is not the result of some strictly empirical process but involves much more—a kind of history of learning.[9]

---

9. For a clear and elaborate presentation of these ideas, see Edward Pols, *Radical Realism* (Ithaca, N.Y.: Cornell University Press, 1998).

A Source of Understanding

One way to know some things is by noticing them within us—an itch, for example, or an ache or a pleasant feeling. When we tell a doctor it hurts someplace, we do this confidently because we can notice things about ourselves without having to stand outside, making publicly confirmable observations. Doctors typically do not answer our reports about pains by rebuffing us with, "Well, but how could you know where it hurts without providing testable evidence of it?"

Nor do the things we notice about ourselves consist only of sensations such as pains or pleasures. We also notice at times that we have a nonworking organ—we cannot hear or see well enough or are numb in certain places. Or, even more complicated, we recall having been someplace or having heard something specific, such as a rumor or a bell that went off in the night. To identify these as what they are, simple sensation—or introspection—alone will not suffice. We need a complex combination of understanding things as things of certain kinds and types.

Thus a narrow understanding of introspection will not help make sense of how we know what happens within us or to us. Rather, introspection has to be understood in a broader sense, as awareness of oneself by oneself with all the cognitive facilities at one's disposal. We are aware of our pain, numbness, sadness, or euphoria by means of understanding, perception, recollection, association, inference, and all the rest. That is, what we come to learn about ourselves does not just rest on our having sensed some things.

Once this is understood, we can then go on to appreciate that we also introspect or become aware of other more complicated things about ourselves. One such thing is that we make choices, decisions, selections, mistakes, and so forth. We often tell others that we are determined to become a doctor or to go to Madagascar for our vacation, that this is something we have decided. Sometimes we report that something we did went wrong because we "didn't think," or that we came up with an answer to a problem because of the thinking we did to solve it. Sometimes we predict that although we do not yet know what we will do, we will think of something when the time comes.

In courts of law, testimony about our awareness of ourselves is often crucial. "When did you know that you no longer loved him?" "What was on your mind when you pulled the trigger?" But for some this is loose, unscientific talk, as though precision is never a matter of life and death in courts of law.

Actually, in the way science proceeds, we make considerable use of self-awareness. We compare what we saw with what others did, and then we report what went on—measurements, clues, indicators, and so forth. Gauges are used to measure distance, time, intensity, and so forth, but we are the ones who record what the gauges indicate and report our awareness, which, by then, has become an item of memory.

We Act Because of Ourselves

So when people report their choices and decisions, it is not at all something undependable that we confront. Instead, we find in such reports what is in common use throughout human experiences. That is one way we learn that people do indeed make choices, often basic ones, which then account for what they do. (My concern here is mainly with these choices or initiatives, in which the role of what is usually called the will comes into play. But I do not thereby wish to claim that there is some object or entity at work here. Rather, I am talking of the beginning point of actions that we human beings take.)

Of course, often people say they were prompted to do this or that by something else. But even then, it is merely prompted, not caused, which usually means that they might have ignored what prompted them but that they chose to heed it instead. Yet, just as we often say such things as, "The car came from that direction," or "The computer knew what to do," we also give abbreviated reports of how people behave. We refer to some fact that they have become aware of and used as a reason to do something, as the cause of what they did. "He became a pianist because of the fine playing of André Watts." "He took up the legal profession because he watched *Perry Mason* in his youth." It makes it appear that these facts just push people around with no initiative of their own involved in what emerges. But the language here is misleading, as before. She took up law maybe because she decided, after watching *Perry Mason* on TV—or reading John Grisham or following *Law and Order* or *The Practice*—that the profession suited her talents, interests, and concerns.

So to discount that people do things on their own, stemming from choices or decisions they have made on their own, is arbitrary or reveals a prejudice based on some philosophical biases or convictions. It must have been something that made him do it. Thus, as an example, Canadian filmmaker Todd Solondz can say, "What excites me, what gets me moving, is trying to look at characters who in any other movie would be the villain or a demon. There is nothing more bracing than in fact trying to dig underneath that veneer and discovering what makes them tick."[10] Although some would perhaps find little in this that contradicts free choice, it does suggest that something makes people be how they are, do what they do, something that we might find and perhaps manipulate so that people act differently. Many social scientists certainly see it this way when they hope for something that can facilitate social engineering.

Our culture is full of such expectations. Underneath evil, there must be something else. This is why psychology, psychiatry, and other soft sciences flourish and why so many defense attorneys are hopeful that they can mount their case in support of someone who is by all appearances guilty, based on some supposed set of events that made him or her behave badly. This is why many social engineers are hopeful that they can manipulate various elements of the social, economic,

10. Quoted in Bernard Weinstein, "At the Movies," *New York Times*, October 1, 1998, B12.

political, educational, or related environment and thereby get people to behave just as they would want them to.

But this does not fit the human situation very well and the disappointments often experienced with social engineering suggest as much. All the problems with utopian political theorizing also support the idea that we are dealing with human nature, which is not quite the same as the nature of other things. These are subject to malleable forces, whereas it is more sensible to identify individual persons as the significant causes of what they do, as agents with their own causal powers. As I write these lines, for example, my thinking is "powered" by myself. When people fail to learn, that, too, seems to be best explained often by reference to their lack of taking initiative and setting out to do something—for example, to focus on an issue, problem, question, or proposal.[11]

And we know this in part because we notice ourselves acting on our own initiative. We decide or fail to do so; we learn or we do not learn; we choose carefully or let things just drift along; we kill or save life; we commit malpractice or act responsibly. And in these and many other such matters it is we who can tell that it is as it is—although often, especially when we are guilty, we choose to hide it and blame it on the stars. Nurture or nature but rarely ourselves!

DETERMINED TO BE DETERMINISTS?

Are We Free to Judge?

A prominent modern version of determinism is that of Laplace. As Bernard Berofsky relates it, it "contends that a knowledge of the mechanical state of all particles at some particular time together with a

---

11. A critic of this work, for example, might surely complain that I have failed to develop a point satisfactorily, that I should have addressed this or that issue more carefully, thus resting on the belief that this is something I might very well have chosen but failed to do.

knowledge of 'all the forces acting in nature' at that instant would enable an intelligence to discover all future and all past states of the world."[12] In simple terms, the world is a daisy chain of events moving from past to future with ineluctable necessity. Thus, whatever we human beings do, we cannot help but do—the past is driving us toward a preset future.

One of the difficulties determinism faces is that, if true, it must be true as well of those who profess the doctrine. Therefore, they would be propounding determinism because they had to do so, just as others who disagree could not do anything else but disagree. And the ascertaining of which doctrine is right would also arise out of necessity.

In other words, since everything happens because it must happen based on what has happened before, the belief in anything happens of necessity, including the belief that determinism is or is not true. The determinist account of human judgment bears on considering determinism itself. By its tenets, we are bound to think whatever we think and that applies to what we think about why we act as we do and whether that thought is true.

Self-Understanding

Yet we tend to view our ordinary reflections on human judgment as a process over which we have a good deal of control. Scientists, jurors, indeed all of us, are expected to control our minds so that considered evidence and logic-based thinking rules, not prejudice.

If the determinist is right, however, we could not engage in independent judgment. Everything would simply be the result of past events, including the assessment of the truth or falsity of determinism. The same would go, of course, for the truth or falsity of a jury verdict, of a scientific finding, or of the worthiness of another human being.

---

12. Bernard Berofsky, "General Introduction," in *Free Will and Determinism* (New York: Harper & Row, 1966), p. 3.

Though ordinarily we would hope that the temptation to prejudge for reasons of color, race, sex, ethnic background, or some other trait would be resisted, this would be impossible if determinism were true.

In commonsense terms, this removes one of the crucial elements from the process of discovering the truth, namely, objectivity. In science, for example, as in law and other areas, it is often insisted that it is best to be objective, not to jump to conclusions but to pay heed to the facts and follow the evidence and argument where they lead. It is vital to clear one's mind of prejudices, preconceptions, and beliefs that might color one's judgment. That way we avoid slanting our conclusions and enable ourselves to learn what we want to know.

Objectivity versus Determinism

Admonitions to be objective, to rid ourselves of preconceptions, and prejudgments, however, have no meaning in a deterministic world in which we, strictly speaking, have no control over what we come to believe. We are made to believe things by forces other than ourselves. Whether we believe determinism is true or false is something not up to our care or lack thereof in the use of our minds. We cannot choose how we approach a subject—we are determined to approach it just as we will.

The determinist's idea of how we come to believe what we believe or say what we say is akin to our ordinary idea of how a computer comes to contain its data and "arguments." We are "programmed" in certain ways, in this case via the forces that operate on our brains and minds. It is much like the way parrots "say" something. They say it because they have to by force of conditioning, not because they have come, on their own accord, to believe it.

By the determinist view, I had to write all of what I just wrote. You had to think all of what you thought upon reading this. It is all a mechanical process or, at most, a series of biochemical, neurological events. The sentences we compose as we think, talk, or write are but the events resulting from certain prior events. We do not produce them, we do not literally compose anything—we simply undergo a complex process, portions being the sentences we think, say, or write.[13]

Some determinists have tried to address this line of argument, of course.[14] They admit the charge that they have to believe what they do. As Adolf Grünbaum notes in defense of determinism, in arguing against the view, "it is first pointed out rightly that determinism implies a causal determination of its own acceptance by its defenders. Then it is further maintained, however, that since the determinist could not, by his own theory, help accepting determinism, he can have no confidence in its truth. Thus it is asserted that the determinist's acceptance of his own doctrine was forced upon him."[15]

What they do not admit, however, is that since this is so, the determination of the truth of determinism is impossible. For the critic says that if we are determined to be determinists, we could never tell whether determinism is true. We would lack the independence or objectivity to examine the issue, since we would be forced to become determinists. Grunbaum objects as follows:

> The causal generation of belief in no way detracts from its reliability. In fact, if a given belief were not produced in us by definite causes, we should have no reason to accept that belief as a concrete description of the world, rather than some other belief arbitrarily selected. Far from making knowledge either adventitious or impossible, the deterministic theory about the origin of our beliefs alone provides

13. The peculiarity of so considering our thinking, speaking, and writing is explored by Edward Pols in *The Acts of Our Being* (Amherst: University of Massachusetts Press, 1982).

14. Adolf Grünbaum, "Causality and the Science of Human Behavior," in Herbert Feigl and May Brodbeck, eds., *Readings in the Philosophy of Science* (New York: Appleton-Century-Crofts, 1953), pp. 766–78.

15. Ibid., p. 775.

the basis for thinking that our judgments of the world are or may be true.[16]

In addition, it is sometimes argued that so long as one is not compelled by someone else to feign accepting a belief, say, determinism, he or she is free and independent and objective enough to reach the determinist conclusion. No other freedom or independence is at issue but what we also ask in science or law or morality: Follow your own judgment, not someone else's. And "your own" judgment means that no one forces you to think, say, or write what you do. It is you who does these things. The fact that you do them because some events have caused you to do them is no obstacle to their being true and reliable. Indeed, how else could you have reached your conclusions apart from certain events leading you to them? Anything else would be arbitrary and capricious, the argument goes.

Being in Charge of Ideas

First, let us note that of nothing else in nature do we say, "They reached their own conclusions, established the truth of the matter," as we do of human beings. Dogs do not know the truth of some proposition, nor do other animals, nor again any computers, despite some metaphorical language that suggests otherwise. Human beings appear to be understood to have that capacity. It is sui generis. It appears that the form of cognitive contact we have with the world—which is called understanding it conceptually—is not found in other animals. This would suggest that there is an intimate connection between the human form of awareness of the world and independent or objective judgment, keeping an open mind as to what we are to conclude about things. And this would suggest that we, unlike other beings that are aware in some

16. Ibid., p. 776.

sense, must be free to form our own judgments, as it were, to cause or produce them.

Second, as you read these lines, you will probably, assuming you make the effort, cause yourself to believe some things about them. They make or do not make sense. They are sound, given the reasoning you see in evidence as you read. They are unclear. They conclusively establish some point, or fail to. (Notice how this resembles the process expected of jurors or scientists or referees and how weighty the result can be!) Are you yourself, over and above the underlying physiological and other prerequisites, not ultimately responsible for the ideas that arise out of this process? Is not a book reviewer achieving something when assessing a book's contents rather than merely serving as a kind of medium undergoing a certain process? And does not reviewing a book assume that the author had a choice as to what ideas, paragraphs, sentences, plot, characterization, arguments, analysis, and so forth, he or she will produce?

Third, Grünbaum has no reason to assert, as he does above, that "the deterministic theory about the origin of our beliefs alone provides the basis for thinking that our judgments are or may be true." He has not examined, at least in this discussion, alternative ways of accounting for or grounding such judgments.

More important, however, he does not consider how we could account for the vast disagreements that also are evident among human beings. These include cases in which people faced with the exact same evidence, presented with the identical arguments, reach different conclusions. Disagreement, in short, seems to make no sense in deterministic terms. Indeed, in the animal world, where it appears instincts do determine behavior, disagreement is not in evidence. All the geese fly south, all the termites set about chewing up the wood. Even among the often-discussed chimps, there is no debate on the merits of bananas.

Starting to Think

Suppose, then, we construe the human mind as a faculty that needs to be given direction, that requires initiation. Then we can at least begin to make sense of disagreement in the face of identical evidence and argument: Some choose to pay full attention, some are careless, some just "aren't there at all." That is exactly what we do, ordinarily. We blame people for missing things because they do not pay heed, are not thinking! We do this with sloppy scientific work; bad verdicts; racial, sexual, or related prejudice; and much of the rest of human misbehavior.

Grünbaum and others seem to be unwilling to extricate themselves from the framework of regarding causes as entirely of the efficient variety. This understandably leads them to suspect any other way of understanding human action besides the deterministic one as irrational, freakish, or weird.

In any case, it looks very much like one simply cannot get away from the notion that we are producing our ideas and are thus responsible for doing it well. Even as one considers this idea, whether it is a good or a bad one, one is doing the thing being talked about.

SHOULD WE BECOME DETERMINISTS?

"Ought" Implies "Can"

James Jordan, among others, has advanced the argument that in defending determinism to others, the determinist faces the dilemma of having assumed that we have free will. I have already made mention of Ted Honderich's rhetorical concluding question in his *How Free Are You?* "[S]hould one part of the response of affirmation be a move to the Left in politics"—in light of what he claims is the truth, namely, that free will does not exist. As noted above, this kind of question about what we ought to or should do falls prey to the famous Kantian motto, "'ought' implies 'can.'" If the question is meaningful, it must be that we have a choice as to what our response will be to learning that we are determined and not free. But then, of course, we are free.

John Kekes—who finds the postulate of initiative incredible— counters this argument by observing that the motto is by no means decisive, since often we think we ought to have done something that turns out not to have been possible to do.[17] We feel a guilt that, as some might put it, is unearned. Skinner and many scientists who endorse what might be called the "freedom is a necessary illusion" thesis lend support to this idea: Despite the apparent implication of freedom from moral discourse, the implication fails to hold. So we need to address Kekes's view before becoming too confident in the power of what has been dubbed the "determinist's dilemma" to undermine the case for determinism.

First, even Kekes does not deny that "'ought' implies 'can'" holds for most cases when we claim that someone ought or ought not to do something. He merely observes that there are exceptions that leave the door open to denying the alleged implication of the motto that we are free if it is meaningful to use "ought to" or "should" in human discourse.

Second, when Kekes argues that there are exceptions to "'ought' implies 'can'"—in cases such as when someone regrets (not) having done something even if there is no way he or she could (not) have done it—a problem arises. Kekes's point places too much weight on what is arguably a special understanding of what could be at issue. Instead of denying "'ought' implies 'can'" on the basis of such rare cases, we might more plausibly explain them as confused thinking, of which

17. John Kekes, "'Ought Implies Can' and Kinds of Morality," *Philosophical Quarterly* 34 (1984): 460–67. See also, his *Facing Evil* (Princeton, N.J.: Princeton University Press, 1991), which includes the bulk of the discussion from the aforementioned paper as well as others, such as "Freedom," *Pacific Philosophical Quarterly* 61 (1980): 368–85.

surely there is ample evidence. One such confusion could be the harboring of false guilt. This is certainly the material of a great deal of serious psychoanalytic thinking. There would be no point in identifying false guilt if there were not instances of genuine guilt. Cases of feeling unjustifiably guilty about what one could not have helped may be genuine, but this implies that there are cases in which the feeling of guilt itself could be justified. This is because we could, on such occasions, have done other than we actually did—saved our child from drug abuse when in fact we neglected to do so or abstained from hurting others when we in fact did choose to hurt them.

Kekes attempts, of course, to develop an alternative analysis based on his contrast between choice and character morality, claiming the latter makes better sense of our moral experiences. The idea seems to be that virtue is not a matter of choosing to do what is right but of behaving in accordance with properly formed character. This sets up an unjustified bifurcation in which one is given the false alternative that virtue involves either choice or character. Yet character-based morality, which I in fact champion, need not be decoupled from initiative. When a child is reared sensibly and thus influenced to develop good character, there could well be the component of self-development, as well, outside of the parental and related influences. A child begins to make choices and, seeing good behavior consistently exhibited by elders and others, cultivates in him- or herself traits that emulate what has been exhibited for him or her. There is no necessity about this, of course. Children of good parents and from good neighborhoods have "gone bad," and it would be tortuous to have to explain this by reference to some fathomed interference. Sometimes the child may have begun to make bad choices despite the best efforts of everyone else to instill good traits. (Here arises the suggestion again that there is something fatally flawed about social engineering.)

One may view Kekes's analysis as making more of ordinary language materials than may be warranted. Indeed, a bit of philosophy may help those caught in such confusion—something that may well be provided by psychotherapists in their somewhat indirect ways, compared with how philosophers would probably make the point to those who may need it but may have to be approached somewhat gingerly.

It is also to be noted that in Kekes's discussion the concept "choice" is used ambiguously: It could mean "selection," as well as "initiation." Yet the idea that human beings have free will requires the latter sense; the former is fully compatible with determinism—animals, as well as anything in motion, may be said to be involved in making selections.

Kekes, in his paper "Freedom," argues for a conception of freedom that involves doing things on one's own, not being forced to do them by other persons. In other words, when one behaves on one's own, one is free. This is where "choice" is used as equivalent to "selection": It was this person, not another, whose behavior exhibited, for example, turning one way rather than another.

Selections are made by many entities. Dogs select the bowl from which to drink or the tree on which to urinate, even though they are impelled to do so and have no choice about the matter in the sense of being the originator of the selection process. Even creeks and rivers select a route toward the lake or sea into which their water flows, but no one thinks they do this of their own free will. The choice that amounts to a selection does not, then, require causal agency, free choice, or initiative.

However, the idea that one initiates the actions one takes—including the mental processes that selection presupposes—is denied by Kekes, who thinks modern science renders this incongruous. As I argue in this book, science does not preclude the initiation of our behavior.

Some Fancy Objections

A similar objection comes from Harry Frankfurter.[18] He argues in support of compatibilism that, when someone would be forced or threatened to do something he or she has already decided to do, the person is doing what ought to be done. Yet because of the impending force or its threat, there is no alternate possibility available, so that "'ought' implies 'can'" is false.

Frankfurter's case is, however, quite contorted, and some work on the details will show that he is wrong. If we say "'ought (to decide)' implies 'can (decide),'" it becomes clear that the claim is true. To say that someone ought to decide to do X rather than Y implies that he or she is free to decide to do X rather than Y, even if no chance actually is afforded to act on the decision. When there is an impending force or threat to do X, this does not affect the point about the availability of the choice to decide. Indeed, that is one reason why sometimes we may praise or blame people who were not able to do other than they did. We learned that they decided to do what is right or what is wrong, granted there was no other option for them but to do one or the other.

Compatibilism, as already noted, is very appealing because it appears to resolve the conflict between two incompatible facts of human life. On the one hand, we seem to be as much a part of nature, which is thought to operate deterministically, as anything else. On the other hand, there also seems to be an inescapable moral dimension to our lives, whereby we act on our own initiative. Compatibilism aims to make room for both of these facts.

Yet there is a problem with the sort of determinism that is embraced by compatibilists. It rules out initiative.[19]

---

18. Harry Frankfurt, "Alternate Possibilities and Moral Responsibility," in Derk Pereboom, ed., *Free Will* (Indianapolis, Ind.: Hackett Publishing Company, Inc., 1997), pp. 156–66.

19. Of course, in a sense my own case is also compatibilist, but not via extending

So, all in all, the point holds up against critics: the advocacy of (mechanistic, efficient-cause type) determinism—which involves making the claim that everyone (who addresses the matter) ought to decide in favor of determinism and against freedom—implies that we are capable of taking the initiative. It does so in what we decide to believe. That is what James Jordan has called "the determinist's dilemma": that to carry on in behalf of determinism, it needs to be conceptually (logically) presupposed that human beings are capable of free choice. This goes to the point that the capacity for initiative is so fundamental in human life that not even the suggestion that we should accept that we lack it can be made coherently without it.

It may be worth noting here that our choices are often long range, as in commitments or promises. So when social scientists find that human action is often predictable, and that some laws of behavior can be formulated that hold for at least statistically significant numbers of cases, this by no means negates the view that human beings have the capacity to initiate their actions. Indeed, a goodly portion of deterministic social science could remain viable despite the falsehood of determinism because when people choose, their choices set them on predictable courses of action.[20]

It bears noting, to conclude this discussion, that many social scientists treat being part of a group with certain convictions as determinism would have to treat being a determinist. They see Democrats, Republicans, militia members, Communists, and others as having been made to think as they do by various factors, including their socioeconomic background and culture. Jury consultants make similar judgments. They look into a prospective juror's background and pre-

---

mechanical determinism to human action and somehow grafting moral responsibility onto it (without genuine free will). Instead, the thesis here is that self-determinism is possible.

20. I argue, in my *Capitalism and Individualism* (New York: St. Martin's Press, 1990), that the social science of economics can be rethought along such foundations. See chapter 14 of that work.

dict his or her views on the defendant's chance for acquittal or conviction.

Determinists would have to have the same view about whether a
person will be a determinist or someone who believes in human initiative and free will. It becomes a matter not of what is true but of how
certain factors have made one think.

WE OFTEN KNOW WE ARE FREE

Is Introspection Valid?

Judgment is something that is entirely yours; it is an element in
personal commitment in an extremely pure state. Because it is so
personal, so much an expression of one's own reasonableness apart
from any constraint, because all alternatives are provided for, it is
entirely one's own responsibility. Because it is entirely one's own
responsibility, one does not complain about one's bad judgments;
one is responsible for them."[21]

In this remark, Bernard Lonegran notes the crux of the free will
thesis advanced in this book: It is because of the nature of (conceptual)
judgment which all bona fide action involves that it is necessary to
conclude that human beings have free will and can initiate their significant conduct. Even before we consider the matter in terms of causality and scientific findings about the human brain, this fact is evident. Indeed, it is because of this fact that before the emergence of the
close scientific study of the brain it was evident enough already that
human beings possess free will. Self-reflection revealed it.

The relevance of introspection is in much disrepute today, however. This is due to several issues, one of which is that it appears to
contradict a famous argument by Ludwig Wittgenstein. He is said to

21. Bernard J. F. Lonegran, *Understanding and Being* (Lewiston, N.Y.: Edwin
Mellen Press, 1980), p. 113; cf. p. 124.

have shown that no one can have a private language, language being a social institution, from which it seems to follow that introspective knowledge is impossible. This is because introspection is supposed to supply a person with data to which only he has access. Thinking and talking about these data could, then, amount to having a private language.

Another reason is that introspection does not give us the kind of publicly accessible knowledge so highly prized in the natural sciences. In short, empiricism appears to be inconsistent with introspection.

Private Language versus Private Data

Regarding the first reservation, if there are private data, there need not be private language. Some things can be available to become known to just one individual, yet the language in which that knowledge is expressed would easily be a social product. One may be alone in knowing where one was sleeping when dreaming about the sweet tea at the ambassador's party, even if talking about the dream and where one had it requires the social medium of language. Still, introspective knowledge sounds very close to being something odd—data about the world that just one person can have. If they are about the world, why could not others also know about them? They can, so introspective knowledge need not be private; it just often is.

And to repeat, there is a lot of it. When on a witness stand, people are often asked to remember things they had not thought of for a while, and they must then search their mind and memory so as to recall them. That is introspective—one needs to inspect some aspect of oneself. When doctors ask you to report on where exactly you have the pain of which you are complaining, once again introspection must be called upon to help out. Even in scientific research, with what might be thought to be quintessentially public data, readers of gauges often require searching their minds to report what they have read. Since much of the awareness human beings obtain of the world is needed after the fact, introspection is required to bring it forth at the right time.

As to empiricism, it has yet to be established as the best theory of human knowledge. Indeed, it seems like a hopeless idea. Clearly we know much that is not based exclusively on observation. And introspection could well involve perceptual knowledge, in any case, obtained by awareness of our various inner constituent components or attributes. So introspection is not in conflict with empiricism, let alone with any more robust conception of human knowledge.

I mention all this so as to help us recall the credibility of introspection. We ask people for what they can produce introspectively, and we often depend on it. We often wish to be sure, as sure as possible, so we back up such reports with others that corroborate them. This only multiplies the reliance on introspection, calling upon many people to make use of it, just in case one or two persons have made mistakes.

Introspective Knowledge of Our Freedom

Often people say they have chosen or decided or set out to do some things, as often as they report that their behavior came about because of various forces working on them. "I hit that car because I was drunk" fits the second description, whereas "I decided to ask her out" fits the first. People are subject to forces that prompt them to behave in various ways—"The flu is making me cough" or "The smog causes me to tear up." And they are also doing things on their own initiative—"I decided to take the thruway instead of Highway 9," "I chose this career instead of that other one." Or, again, "I failed to think about it, so I didn't do it"; "I decided to enroll in history and drop English for this semester"; or "I repeatedly chose to pass the cars that drove ahead of me."

What are we to make of such claims? Are they all false?

If determinism is true in the sense that no one could do other than what he or she does in fact, then these reports cannot be right. They are, as Skinner might put it, prescientific ways of talking about human behavior.[22] Yet, if that is so, all the credibility of introspective reports is called into question. For if we are so deluded about what is going on when we tell about our having chosen or decided to do this or that, this casts suspicion on the other reports we make about ourselves. What is suggested by the Skinnerian idea is that things make us give certain reports, just as they make us behave in certain ways, and we have nothing to do with either in any decisive way.

DOES KNOWLEDGE PRESUPPOSE INITIATIVE?

To Know We Must Think Free

The idea is not difficult to appreciate: A prerequisite for knowledge proper is that we are not compelled in what we come to know. Both the cases of scientific and judicial objectivity, at least as serious goals we can reach, rest on this implicit view. If one's mind is forced to reach conclusions, if it lacks independence as one examines evidence and arguments, then objectivity and thus knowledge of reality are barred. That is the story to be explored here. Is this right? Or is Adolf Grünbaum correct to argue that determinism, hard or soft, does not undermine objective knowledge?

We have seen already that the kind of freedom or liberty that is taken by many to be a precondition of ethics—"'ought' implies 'can'"—is supposed to be found in or around the human form of consciousness—thoughtfulness, thinking, mindfulness. Kant, Strauss, Wittgenstein, and Rand all share this conviction: If there is to be

22. B. F. Skinner, *Beyond Freedom and Dignity* (New York: Bantam Books, 1972); *Science and Human Behavior* (New York: Macmillan, 1953). See Tibor R. Machan, *The Pseudo-Science of B. F. Skinner* (New Rochelle, N.Y.: Arlington House Publishing Company, 1974), for a criticism of Skinner's ideas.

genuine freedom of choice, human initiative, it must be in the region of human life in which judgment, planning, theorizing, even the most simple conceptual awareness, are conducted.

Here is how this may be grasped: To act beyond simple movement involves more and more complex judgment. "I will go to church and pray for my soul," or "Let us send a space vehicle to Mars and retrieve some rocks so we may study them," or "My wife and I will go to counseling to see what we can do about the trouble in our home" all require one to form a judgment that will guide the behavior that is to fulfill the purpose or end at hand. Abstract ideas, which make up the judgment—concepts, principles, theories, probabilities, estimates, even intelligent guesses—are not provided to us by our genes or instincts. There is a constant growth of such ideas, so the bulk of them are not present when someone's biological identity is formed. One needs to learn ideas, principles, theory, and so forth, and, as teachers are wont to observe, learning requires some measure of initiative, paying attention, coming to "grasp" what is what. As John Locke noted, "[T]hough we cannot hinder our knowledge where the agreement is once perceived, nor our assent, where the probability manifestly appears upon due consideration of all the measures of it; yet we can hinder both knowledge and assent, by stopping our inquiry, and not employing our faculties in the search of any truth. If it were not so, ignorance, error, or infidelity could not in any case be a fault."[23] This cuts very deep, for if what we think about the very issue we are discussing is false, no resolution can be reached, for everyone would be equally right or wrong, a conclusion no one could hope to ascertain any better than anyone else, reaching thus a standoff at best, or more likely nonsense.

This picture of the human mental life furthermore explains, better than does a deterministic one, that knowledge can be cumulative, that

---

23. John Locke, *Essay in Human Understanding* (New York: World Publishing Company, 1964), p. 440.

we can be taught and then take what we have learned and build on it without each one of us having to experience what underpins this knowledge. Whereas some animals show a modicum of such capacity, human life is largely dependent upon it for its survival and flourishing.

This view of the human mind also makes the best sense of ordinary expressions such as "I should have thought," "Damn it, I didn't think," "Think before you act," and so forth. It fits better with the idea that at some point for each adult person an ultimate accountability or responsibility is reached in our faculty of conceptual consciousness. It bears on our proceedings throughout our conscious life, even as we consider the issue we are here discussing, for some people will say that a philosophical adversary has not thought something through sufficiently, some will claim that another has failed to heed some points, and so forth, all of which require the conception of human initiative so as to make sense.

This also gives support to an epistemologically oriented conception of ethics: We are responsible for the quality of our consciousness, the shape of our ideas and principles. As Barry Stroud puts it in a much more explicitly epistemological context, laying out Wittgenstein's idea of conceptual development:

> [logical necessity] is not like rails that stretch to infinity and compel us always to go in one and only one way; but neither is it the case that we are not compelled at all. Rather, there are the rails we have already traveled, and we can extend them past the present point only by depending on those that already exist. In order for the rails to be navigable they must be extended in smooth and natural ways; how they are to be continued is to that extent determined by the route of those rails that are already there.[24]

24. Barry Stroud, "Wittgenstein and Logical Necessity," in I. G. Pitcher, ed., *Wittgenstein* (Garden City, N.Y.: Anchor Books, 1966), p. 496.

Then Stroud adds that he has "been primarily concerned to explain the sense in which we are 'responsible' for the ways in which the rails are extended, without destroying anything that could properly be called their objectivity."[25] The idea strongly implicit here is that it is in the realm of forming our concepts that we have the liberty and responsibility to do the right thing, but not as a matter of some automatic process that "compel[s] us always to go in one and only one way." Rather, we are responsible for how the rails are laid but in line with certain standards that the laying of past rails and other facts about rails have established.

This idea, that concept formation presupposes the capacity for human initiative, counts significantly against a fully deterministic account of human conduct. As noted already, even the giving of an account presupposes the idea: That is why a critic's scrutiny makes sense, since it can uncover infelicities that could have been avoided. When Kant found freedom as the condition enjoyed by the human will, it is because the will is the engine of intention and reason, which must be subject to responsibility lest one be guilty of moral wrongdoing.

Wittgenstein makes the point, too, that it is thinking that makes someone a good human being. He says, in a letter to Paul Engelmann, "I work diligently enough but wish that I were better and wiser. And these two things are the same."[26] As noted above, this is a conception of human moral goodness that we find widely considered, by Socrates, Aristotle, Spinoza, Kant, and, especially, Ayn Rand. It suggests that both our basic capacity for freely acting and the responsibility to act rightly are accountable by reference to our role, via the faculty of our mind, as self-directed agents who must take the initiative to do well at

25. Ibid.
26. Wittgenstein to Paul Engelmann, *Letters from Ludwig Wittgenstein. With a Memoir* (March 31, 1917), ed. B. F. McGuinnes (London: Oxford University Press, 1967), S. 4.

living. No instincts, drives, built-in motives, evolutionary forces, or laws of history will produce what is most important for us, namely, our own successful living, flourishing, or human excellence.

What seems to be missing in all this, however, is room for explaining and predicting human conduct. If what people do is a matter of their own choice or determination, how can we explain their actions, let alone predict them?

If initiative is conceived along lines offered in this book, as self-determination, the explanation of human action would have to include the agent's choice or decision as an irreducible element. Why did Mozart produce such beautiful music? In part, because he decided to devote himself to that task. That is one element of the explanation that cannot be dispensed with. It is Mozart himself who made the music and made it what it is, beautiful.

This, of course, is just how we often explain historical events, by reference to the choices made by the figures who have made a significant difference in how history unfolds. Alexander the Great, Napoleon, Karl Marx, Lenin, Hitler, Churchill, and others, chose to think and act in certain ways, which, in part, explains how things turned out. In less than the grandiose matters of human affairs, too, we explain how things turn out by reference to such human choices. When we discuss why a couple has divorced, why a young person entered a certain career, or why a book sold so well, we make references to the decisions and choices of—that is, the initiative taken by—the individuals involved.

There is a similar pattern to how we predict human events. We refer to what people have decided to do, to their short- and long-term commitments, flowing from their initiative. Indeed, the social sciences, which seek explanation for human events, could continue without a hitch by incorporating this feature of human life, provided it is recognized that initiative can be sustained long term, as in the commitment to be faithful to one's spouse or to pursue a career conscientiously. The economist, for example, who believes that in order to uphold standards of science it is necessary to assume that human behavior is explained and predictable by virtue of various forces that determine such behavior need not give up the scientific standing of the discipline. Instead of holding that only forces apart from the person can count as explanatory factors, it could be taken as an explanatory factor that a person made a decision to, say, enter the market and seek out good deals. Although this may not hold out the promise of a total explanation, neither does the alternative, given that few social scientists believe they can lay their hands on all the relevant variables as they explain and predict what people do. Statistical predictions are certainly equally possible with the element of personal self-determination and commitment included in the explanatory scheme as compared with ones wherein such a determinant is left out.

We can, then, conclude that the framework of human understanding wherein initiative is a significant factor need not be consigned to the antiscientific domain. That is what Pinker and others accept. But that is not necessary so as to make room for the role of the mind as a causal determinate of human action. Human beings exert initiative, and this, in part, explains what happens to them and how the world turns out around them. Their commitments to certain policies, their loyalty, and so forth also make predicting what they will do and how things will happen a real prospect.

IS INITIATIVE WEIRD?

Strange Powers?

Robert Kane has noted a central deficiency of the libertarian[27] tradition on the free-will question:

---

27. The term "libertarian" is often associated with political philosophy, signifying an order wherein the right to individual liberty is the central public good that the law is supposed to secure. However, it is also the term often used to signify the view that human beings have free will and can act on their own initiative.

[It has] invoked factors such as noumenal selves, transempirical power centers; Cartesian egos; special "acts of will"; "acts of attention" or "volition" that cannot in principle be determined; mental events that exist outside of (but can also intervene within) the natural order; special forms of agent, or non-occurrent, causation that cannot be accounted for in terms of familiar kinds of event or occurrent causation; the "Will" conceived as a kind of uncaused homunculus within the agent; and so on.[28]

The free-will position I have been spelling out and defending does indeed rest in part on—or at least invokes in its support—the idea that a form of causation is found in nature other than the "familiar kinds of event or occurrent causation." Yet, if it is indeed the case that different kinds of causes—depending on what type or kind of being is involved in a causal relationship—exist in reality, there is nothing mysterious about them, incomparable to noumenal selves or Cartesian egos. And the list above should also exclude "acts of will" and "acts of attention," provided these are understood in naturalist ways, fitted within the framework of the natural order of reality.

Although Kane is right that "it has been all too tempting for libertarians to look for those additional factors in mysterious sources outside the natural order or to postulate unusual forms of agency or causation whose manner of influence on events is at best obscure,"[29] he is wrong to lump with such efforts the latter kind. To claim, with Aristotle and others, that causation is not all of the same type is not to invoke anything mysterious, unless one prejudges all nonempiricist, nonreductivist accounts of causation as mysterious.

Aristotle argued that being, although uniting everything by way of its basic laws—the law of noncontradiction, for example—is also quite diverse. Different types or categories of beings are found throughout

28. Robert Kane, *The Significance of Free Will* (London: Oxford University Press, 1998), p. 115.
29. Ibid.

nature. Analogously, different types or categories of causes may well be found, also, throughout nature, especially if a cause is understood to emanate from the nature of what is involved in causal relations. So a pebble will exhibit different causal relationships from a beaver or a human being, because all these are essentially different from one another.

In short, initiative is not weird, but a type of causal action that can be exhibited by beings of a certain kind, ones with the faculty of conceptual consciousness, ones able to produce ideas, theories, artifacts, and fictional and other imaginary mental entities. That such creative, original actions exhibit a form of causation different in type from what billiard balls or planets or even electrons exhibit when they collide should certainly not be deemed necessarily mysterious, unless we prejudge nature to contain only efficient causation.

Kane points out that invoking this type of causation has bothered some of its proponents. For example, Richard Taylor, who once defended what is called "agent-causation," noted that "One can hardly affirm such a theory of agency with complete comfort . . . and wholly without embarrassment, for the conception of men and their powers which is involved in it is strange indeed, if not positively mysterious."[30]

I do not see at all why any embarrassment need face someone who embraces the idea of agent causation (including the more basic idea that causes can be entities or beings, not events or occurrences only), any more than such embarrassment need face someone who embraces the idea that human life is unique enough to include free will of any kind or such creative capacities as are involved in composing music, writing novels, or establishing educational or political institutions. There is novelty in the various forms of being, certainly in life and

30. Richard Taylor, *Metaphysics* (Englewood Cliffs, N.J.: Prentice-Hall, 1974), p. 58. For Taylor's elaborate defense of agent-causation, see Richard Taylor, *Action and Purpose* (Englewood Cliffs, N.J.: Prentice-Hall, 1966).

especially in human life. There are serious differences between electrons and molecules, cells and thinking brains, even fish and birds.

What is so mysterious about the supposition that at the human level of life a form of causality is present that is not found elsewhere, at least not prominently (although higher mammals may well exhibit it, too)? If, moreover, the supposition of such causation is reasonable from a metaphysical standpoint, phenomenologically plausible, and also manages to explain better than other suggestions the immense variety of human activities and institutions—cultures, religions, political organizations, and so forth—why should it be construed as strange?

Moreover, as suggested earlier, agent causation need not be confined to human behavior. In many animal life forms there is sufficient inventiveness, even originality, involving some measure of mentality beyond the purely reactive kind, so that efficient causation is insufficient to account for all of it. To complain, furthermore, that agent-causality—in other words, human initiative—fails to have explanatory power is to fail to appreciate that it is an individual who produces the initiative. It is Mozart whose existence and choices explain his works, not some force apart from him nor his wishes or reasoning or desires, since it is Mozart who forms wishes, engages in reasoning, and cultivates desires.[31] The ultimate responsibility that Kane and others rightly insist on linking with human initiative lies within the individual. It is the individual who can and does, at most times, take the

31. This view is laid out in great detail in Edward Pols, *The Acts of Our Being* (Amherst: University of Massachusetts Press, 1982). The underlying metaphysics here is laid out by H.W.B. Joseph in his *An Introduction to Logic* (Oxford University Press, 1906), pp. 401ff. Joseph calls attention to the idea that causes are beings or entities in, for example, the following passage: "the earth is not more antecedent than consequent in time to the movement of a pendulum which it attracts; and oxygen and hydrogen are ingredients necessary to the formation of water, but they do not happen like their combination. Cause no doubt implies change and succession. But there can be no change without something which changes, i.e., which persists through a succession of states." (p. 405)

initiative to use his or her mind to form ideas, plans, theories, images, and so forth. These are what develop into reasons, wishes, desires, and the like that are classifiable into various kinds in an effort to distinguish between different ways human individuals come to do what they do—direct armies, conduct orchestras, raise children, write novels, design clothing, imagine ideal lovers, or formulate philosophical theories.

To argue that the cause of all this is no different from the cause that produces earthquakes or atomic blasts is to force upon us a reductionism that is far more weird than agent causation would ever be. And Kane seems to appreciate some of this when he notes that nonoccurrent causation may well be needed not just for libertarian theory but for, say, action theory in general. He himself tries to do without such causation, which is a fine effort but one that seems to bend over backward toward satisfying the reductionist philosophical tradition of explanation by reference to event causation alone. Such an effort is plagued by all of what plagues reductionism—for example, the inability to account for wide differences in nature, including how various diverse results are produced by natural (especially living and, primarily, human) beings. So it is much better to make the case for free will or human initiative without accepting the framework the terms of which Kane wishes to satisfy.

In short, free will—in the sense that human beings can initiate some of their significant behavior—is not weird because nature makes possible, indeed, includes many kinds of beings that differ from one another significantly. Thus nature can just as readily include a kind of being that causes its own behavior and exhibits initiative as it can ones that do not. So long as there is no implication of some contradiction in nature—between the plethora of efficient causal relationships and the relatively limited (to the human sphere) range of causes of agent causation—there is reason to seriously consider the existence of a new type of cause. It is certainly no more unusual than is language, meaning, music, libraries, engineering, or philosophy.

MODERN SCIENCE AND INITIATIVE

Science and Metaphysics

When philosophers and others defend determinism, often they think it is science that demands this. They hold that a proper science of human behavior must be wedded to the idea that human beings behave because the laws of nature require them to do it. And that means for most of them that some events must cause what we do. Without this no science of human behavior exists.

B. F. Skinner was perhaps the most ardent promulgator of this view. But others are not far behind him. Yet some exceptions exist. Among them, perhaps, Roger W. Sperry was the most famous, a recipient of the Nobel Prize in medicine in 1958 and a proponent of the view that it is not science but a questionable metaphysics that has led to the widespread embrace of determinism.[32]

Once the metaphysical nature of determinism is understood, we can ask just what science requires in the way of a rational explanation of human behavior. And here the answer could be provided in terms of different kinds of causes. Their nature would, in turn, depend on the kind of behavior we want explained. Billiard balls, of course, do behave along lines spelled out by (mechanistic) determinists. The mating habits of cats may not be explainable in the same fashion by reference only to mechanical causes. And what Mozart, Van Gogh, Aristotle, and George Washington did would invite yet another type of causal explanation—self-determination.

32. Roger W. Sperry, *Science and Moral Priority* (New York: Columbia University Press, 1983). See also his "Changing Concepts of Consciousness and Free Will," *Perspectives in Biology and Medicine* 9 (August 1976): 9–19.

Downward Causation

Sperry has identified what he has dubbed "downward" causation
in several realms of nature, and one example of it can be found in how
the faculty of human mentality guides what human beings do. The
idea is that the structure of an entity or organism may provide it with
powers that enable it to do some things on its own. Thus it is because
of what bees are that a bee is able to make honey. And given the kind
of being humans are, we can think. Thinking being what it is, namely,
a necessarily creative, originating activity (since ideas are not found
in nature but must be developed by thinking beings), human beings
have the capacity to do something original. Given how much such
thinking factors into their lives—how each action they take involves
judgment, planning, conceptualization—this element of origination is
part of their nature.

Various experiments recounted by Sperry appear to bear out his
account of human mentality.[33] Sperry makes the point this way in one
of his discussions:

> we can say in summary that it is possible to see today an objective,
> explanatory model of brain function that neither contradicts nor
> degrades but rather affirms age-old humanist values, ideals, and
> meaning in human endeavors. The noble, free, or heroic, the exalted
> or sublime, qualities—or the opposite, for that is how meanings
> arise—that the humanist formerly thought he could see in man and
> his activities are present in our model.[34]

This line of analysis is very similar to the broader theory laid out
by Edward Pols. He first shows that the purely empiricist scientific
method is unsound, and whenever deployed, relies on much that is not

33. Ibid.
34. Roger W. Sperry, "Mind, Brain, and Humanist Values," in John R. Platt, ed.,
New Views of the Nature of Man (Chicago: University of Chicago Press, 1965), p. 92.

included in the usual statements that describe it. In other words, even so-called empirical science is not what it is said to be, reliance upon nothing but the evidence of the senses. The activity of the scientist is such that we learn from it that science is anything but purely empirical. Indeed, Pols shows in several of his discussions just how thinking and talking about the controversy itself belies the empiricist-materialist account of human behavior. There is no way to explain how sentences and paragraphs gain their meaning and how they would lack it when incomplete without conceiving of their creation as a type of origination or initiation.

Others, too, have noted that modern science needs a different account of human behavior from the classical mechanical sort that has been in vogue for several centuries. Not all provide the same alternative, but there is a growing literature of skepticism about the standard model, as it were.[35]

And surely there needs to be. To think that the way billiard balls cause the movement of other billiard balls is how beavers build dams or black widow spiders reproduce, not to mention how Mozart or Joyce create their art works, is quite unjustified by anything in any discipline of science.[36] Indeed, the idea of materialism cannot stand much philosophical scrutiny, given that "matter" is not some additional stuff in reality. At its best the concept means the manifold of persistent stuff that manifests itself in innumerable ways throughout reality. You, I, the lamp, the apple in the kitchen, the rainbow, or the marks on my computer all consist of some material, an aspect of itself that persists without extinction and conforms to the basic laws of being. The conservation of mass and energy, for example, applies to matter—the stuff of everything.

But matter isn't some being itself that lies at the bottom of it all. What lies there is the myriad of beings themselves, of which the prin-

---

35. Jon Eccles, *The Understanding of the Brain* (New York: McGraw-Hill, 1977).
36. Machan, *The Pseudo-Science of B. F. Skinner.*

ciple of their lack of total extinction is one. Things change into other things, beings into other beings, and so forth. They do not get wiped out, extinguished. But that principle does not hold because some one kind of being is present in everything. Rather it holds because no thing can come from nothing and no thing can become nothing.

In the social sciences, too, the idea that crime, divorce, adolescent confusion, midlife crises, and the like do not happen to us but that our initiative in part accounts for these is now a live option. The self-esteem movement in psychology clearly presupposes that human beings may earn credit for their achievements and need to acknowledge this, to gain psychological sustenance from it. The Freudian and Skinnerian determinists are no longer the standard-bearers in the field, although because of the strong momentum of scientism, much of experimental psychology harks back to their legacy.

In any case, contemporary science does not lack support for the idea that human brain physiology and psychology are not just compatible with but support human initiative.

THE BEST THEORY IS TRUE

Truth

A part of discussing any complex idea is to figure out how it might be shown to be true. It is simple enough to tell if there really are four chairs in the dining room, if there are an even 250 million citizens in some country, or whether the sun is out or behind clouds this day. But whether determinism or free will is the truth about the way human beings behave is not so simple. There seem to be good arguments given on both sides of the debate, and there are also some rather complicated claims that may be tough to defend. Ambiguities, vagueness, and other problems can plague the inquiry.

The very idea of truth may need to be examined so as to figure out which theory ought to be assented to. And that is what I wish to do here before moving on to the second major area of this work, namely, indicating the relevance of the controversy of political theory and public policy.

The Best Theory Is True

I wish to defend the idea that when we put all of the points made thus far together we get a more sensible understanding of the complexities of human life than we do otherwise. We get a better understanding, for example, of why social engineering and government regulation and regimentation do not work, why there are so many individual and cultural differences, why people can be wrong, why they can disagree with each other, and so forth. It is because they are free, not set in some pattern.

Furthermore, in principle, all of the behavior of these creatures around us can be predicted. They are not creative in a sense that they originate new ideas and behavior, although we do not always know enough about the constitution of these beings and how it would interact with their environment to actually predict what they will do. Human beings produce new ideas, and these can introduce new kinds of behavior in familiar situations. This, in part, is what is meant by the fact that different people often interpret their experiences differently. Yet we can make some predictions about what people will do because they often do make up their minds in a given fashion and stick to their decisions over time. This is what we mean when we note that people make commitments, possess integrity, and so forth. So we can estimate what they are going to do. But even then we do not make certain predictions but only statistically significant ones.

Is Free Will Well Founded?

Free will explains, much better than do deterministic theories, how human life involves such a wide range of possibilities—accomplishments as well as defeats, joys as well as sorrows, creation as well as destruction. It also explains why in human life there is so much change—in language, custom, style, art, and science. Unlike other living beings, for which what is possible is fixed by instincts and reflexes, people initiate much of what they do, for better and for worse.

To summarize again, concerning the distinctly ontological presuppositions of moral responsibility—indeed, of any responsibility for any kind of conduct—the above line of argument suggests that sometimes we learn about ontology via what has been called "the inference from best explanation." Free will is a capacity of a certain entity to do certain things, to choose. But because once a choice is made the direct evidence confirms only one of the alternatives, the capacity for such a choice cannot be verified by that kind of evidence.

However, in many areas of human inquiry—science (black holes), criminal law (*mens rea*), motivational psychology (subconscious intentions)—we learn of what there is by means of such arguments. So it would not be out of place to show that there is an ontological fact, namely, free will, that underlies human moral responsibility. The evidence, and its proper analysis, leaves no other reasonable conclusion to be reached.

CHAPTER TWO

Why Worry about Freedom?

VARIETIES OF FREEDOM

It is always useful to be reminded of just why we care about human liberty. The issue can never go away—every new generation needs to consider its significance and ramifications.

The concept of "freedom" or "liberty" has many uses and senses, and they are all relevant to our controversies and problems in political life, as well as to our aspirations as individuals. The sort of liberty at issue in politics is the liberty not to have people intruding on each other's lives nor encroaching upon one another's sovereignty. The sort of liberty at issue in one's private life is the capacity to act on one's own initiative, without being driven to act by forces outside oneself. Both of these are vital, and they are also related. For example, in criminal justice, if one has not personally chosen to do the crime, the idea that one should be punished for it will not make much sense. Nor will respect for individual sovereignty and autonomy make much difference if we lack self-direction in our lives.

There are some who deny this, as we have seen, mainly, I think, because they are concerned that the complexities of the free-will problem will infect those of political economy. It is best to keep them separate. That way we can at least make headway with the latter, even if the former remains an enigma.

But there is no way to avoid the connection. We complain about the loss of political or economic liberty, but if there is no human initiative, then this loss is inevitable. Tyrannies, oppression, violations of rights, government and criminal misconduct, and the rest are all just like natural disasters, happenings over which we can do no more than some hand-wringing. If human beings do what they do because the forces of nature drive them to do it, then only fate is responsible when they do political or criminal wrongs. This may put the matter too plainly for some of those who have been addressing the issue, but there is no escaping the simple conclusion. "Que sera, sera" still says it best—what will be, will be.

CONNECTING LIBERTIES

So are the two liberties connected? And how are they?

I begin with a passage from an interview with John Kenneth Galbraith. He is not usually thought to be a champion of individual liberty, not at least in the sense in which it will be considered here.

Galbraith is asked, in an Italian magazine interview, as follows: "You spoke of the failure of socialism. Do you see this as a total failure, a counterproductive alternative?" He replies this way: "I'd make a distinction here. What failed was the entrepreneurial state, but it had some beneficial effect. I do not believe that there are any radical alternatives, but there are correctives. The only alternative, socialism, that is the alternative to the market economy, has failed. The market system is here to stay."[1]

Galbraith was the second major American socialist thinker—the

---

1. See the October 1996 in-flight magazine *Alitalia*.

other being Robert Heilbroner[2]—who has publicly thrown in the towel, as it were. Both still advocate some version of the meddling state, so let us not regard their change of mind as a serious enlightenment.

Clearly, however, both were in retreat for a while after the collapse of the Soviet socialist empire. Since then, they have been concerned about how to salvage something of the all-promising but basically inept state in the face of the onslaught of the philosophy of freedom. (This ineptness stems not from some basic evil on the part of politicians but from being faced with impossible tasks, such as trying to make people be good![3])

There is a pattern of statist failures, of disasters in the wake of the failure to respect freedom. Even as the faithful try everything to keep the powerful state in business, this failure keeps asserting itself. To understand it, however, we have to explore freedom itself, see how it fits with our lives as human beings. We know one thing at the outset, though—or some of us do. This is that the failure of socialism and other systems is not some accident, something that could not be avoided, something people were powerless to prevent. And this fact makes the connection between political economy and free will (or human initiative) clear.

HUMAN NATURE AT ISSUE

To explain why this connection is unavoidable, we first must examine human nature itself. It is by reference to what something is that we can learn what it is capable of doing. By knowing what apples are,

2. Robert Heilbroner, "After Communism," *New Yorker* (September 10, 1990): 92.
3. Interesting efforts in defending such a role for the state can be found in James P. Sterba, *How to Make People Just* (Lanham, Md.: Rowman and Littlefield, 1988) and Robert P. George, *Making Men Moral* (London: Oxford University Press, 1995).

we can tell that they are capable of serving as nourishment for human beings and that they are not likely to be complicit in soiling the rug in one's apartment. The nature of something is that which makes it what it is—that is why there is such concern about human nature, the nature of government, of crime, of mental disease, and of AIDS.[4]

True, the idea often calls to mind Plato's theory of forms. Therein the natures of things are taken to be final, perfect, and true statements of what is being considered (virtue, knowledge, or justice). And this aspiration cannot be met, so it is fuel for skepticism, according to which no knowledge of natures is possible.

Yet there are less rigid and more plausible conceptions of what it is to be the nature of something, ones in which both stability and flexibility or development, even improvement, can be accommodated.[5] Knowing human nature should help to discover why violating human liberty gives rise to failure, why it brings mostly disaster, why even the few achievements that follow on its heels are paid for so dearly that the prize is never worth the price.

Political liberty—not having others usurp one's sovereignty, one's role as the governor of one's life—is a precondition for civil life, not just a bourgeois class preference. Preferences are just that—they are not needed, not even firmly wanted, only something that some people wish for and others can do without. It is evident, though, from both analysis and experience, that one cannot just dispense with freedom.

Why is that so? What is it about human beings that requires that they be granted this fundamental condition by other people? Why do millions of people want, consistently, to have their own status as initiators—as creators, as originators, as something other than wallflow-

---

4. This idea is developed in full in Edward Pols, *The Acts of Our Being* (Amherst: University of Massachusetts Press, 1983).

5. See also Tibor R. Machan, *Individuals and Their Rights* (LaSalle, Ill.: Open Court Publishing Company, 1989). For a promising defense of the nature of definitions, see Ayn Rand, *Introduction to Objectivist Epistemology* (New York: Meridian, 1990).

ers—respected? Even when they cave in, quite inconsistently, to certain pleas for coercion or intrusiveness, they cannot stand it very long. They change their minds and demand this fundamental condition of being treated as creative original beings. Why is that so?

Almost any other animal has a facility for succumbing to a state of servitude. They can be domesticated, eventually, with a little behavior modification. But human beings seem unable to adjust for very long to a condition of servitude. They may be defeated in their resistance by more powerful people and a sustained tradition of subjugation, but despite certain long periods of such repression that might have squelched all efforts at it, resistance to violating individual liberty has been nearly universal throughout human history. This is not an accident.

In order to get a start on answering the question of why freedom matters, it is not too difficult to find a laboratory because we are dealing with ourselves. We can observe ourselves directly at every moment of our waking hours. Our lives are the laboratories.

Every reader can check the truth for him or herself of some of the things I say here. This is as it should be, because there are no special experts on this topic, only individuals who choose to address it more or less intensely in their own lives.

OUR CREATIVE INITIATIVE

The first thing that you can notice is that, as you are reading or listening to anyone, you are or could be making a critical judgment. You are engaging in something active, not just responsive, not just passive. You are doing more than just noticing a smell, registering a sight. You are giving meaning to things, not arbitrarily, not capriciously; you are the one who is identifying the meaning of your world. That is a creative, inventive act, no mere automatic reaction.

In short, human beings can always take a first step, bringing something about that has not been there before. This is the quintessential aspect of human existence, the primary thing that distinguishes us from so many other entities in nature.

In many respects we are, of course, just like dogs and cats and giraffes. If we are cut, we bleed. We all have to eat. We are, indeed, very much like the rest of the animals, except that we do not seem to have many of their limitations, nor their abundant built-in attributes for staying alive and, especially, for flourishing. We alone need to take the initiative to learn how to do this. In order for us to make any headway in life—be it art, science, philosophy, automotive engineering, cooking, or raising children—we, individually, must make the effort to be there, to address the matter, to attend—not to stand by idly, but to pay attention.

This sort of personal, individual initiative is something that other living things do not make use of. Yes, there are some borderline cases in which some evidence for nonhuman animal initiative exists: You can put an ape into a laboratory and squeeze from it some awareness of this kind. But it is no necessity of life for apes as it is for us. We do not live very well, nor very long, if we do so passively. Even if we do, such passive survival means some form of parasitism, dependence on someone else's active engagement with the world.

This element of initiative that is so crucial to human existence and human flourishing is the first type of freedom that I want to identify here. It is what is usually referred to as free will and means that we are in charge of some of the vital things we do.

So we, individually, are the ones who take the ultimate initiative in life. But that idea is a very controversial one throughout the history of philosophy. Over the last four hundred years especially it has been extremely difficult to sustain a case for free will. One reason for the importance of the eighteenth-century German philosopher Immanuel Kant is that he found some way of making room for free will in the midst of an intellectual era in which it was largely precluded by everything that people were beginning to believe. The mechanistic world, the world of Isaac Newton, certainly did not leave much room for the idea that there could be something in nature that could take the initiative, that could move on its own power, as it were. (Newton did ascribe this power to God, though.)

SCIENCE VERSUS LIBERTY

To reiterate some of the points already covered earlier in this book, this is a very difficult issue to think about even in our time. Many social scientists, including economists, have a hard time fathoming the notion that human beings do not behave exactly as does much of the rest of nature—reacting to pressures they experience—but have the capacity to act freely. Certainly we can see, wherever we live, that the culture widely embraces the idea that we are moved and do not act. (The very idea of "motive" arises from that idea.)

In contrast, the notion of individual responsibility is passé, especially the way many experts see the situation. Thus, for example, in his book *Nature, Nurture, and Chance*, Peter M. Rinaldo chronicles the lives of three Canadian brothers and explicitly confines himself to an "exploration of [the influences of] genetics, birth order, and chance on their lives."[6] We are all victims, as the saying goes—yet the idea of victim does not even make sense in that context because a victim needs a culprit, something that is impossible without free will.[7] There cannot be culprits in a fully mechanistic world. We are all just billiard balls moved around by the forces that shove us. So "casualty" would be a better term to use to designate all those who have encountered

6. Peter N. Rinaldo, *Nature, Nurture, and Chance: The Lives of William, Edward, and Peter Trout* (Briarcliff Manor, NY: Dorpete Press, 1998). The quote is from an advertisement for the work that appeared in the *New York Review of Books* (February 5, 1998): 21.

7. For more on this point, see Tibor R. Machan, "Rescuing Victims—from Social Theory," in D. Sank & D. I. Caplan, eds., *To Be a Victim* (New York: Plenum Press, 1991), and chapter 3 of this work.

mishaps in their lives, casualties of the various ineluctable forces of nature.

This view, from which Kant could only break by dividing the world into two parts—one in which it holds firmly and another in which freedom reigns—seemed very sensible for a long time, because certain areas of nature certainly seemed to be very much in accord with that perspective. And, indeed, by recognizing the mechanical forces of the world, we managed very well to manipulate nature to our own purposes. The entire industrial revolution and the massive advances of technology testify to the usefulness of looking at some of nature from the Newtonian framework.

So, once again, we can see the impetus, emotional and intellectual, for wishing to carry that idea much further. Social engineering is the most crucial extension, as well as perhaps the most misguided result, of this effort.

The extrapolation from astronomy and from classical mechanics into the area of human affairs was done quite innocently. It promised to be a way to solve problems. Among other things, debilitating diseases, deprivation, distance, and other obstacles to human living came to be subject to successful manipulation because of this new scientific—actually scientistic—understanding of human life. Poverty was widely abated, comfort was secured, work was made more enjoyable, human life improved considerably. So the scientistic mentality cannot be dismissed as mere trifle, some kind of unwise hubris, as some contend. It has profound, although inconsistent, implications for how politics and public policy are conceived.[8]

---

8. The inconsistency stems from, on the one hand, the wish to apply the mechanistic engineering model to shaping society and, on the other, implicitly rejecting it in urging that citizens choose, via the political process, its application. (For more on this point, see chapter 3.)

SCIENTISM, NOT SCIENCE PROPER

The trouble is, it was a hurried action, the consequence of a hasty generalization: the fallacy of thinking that just because some entities in nature are under the jurisdiction of the principles of classical mechanics therefore all of them must be. Not even in all of physics does this appear to be true.

When we consider that the human brain is probably the most complicated entity in the universe, it is not surprising that it exhibits certain principles that are fundamentally different from what other things in nature exhibit. But that realization came only recently and only from some dissenting scientists. One had to have had great confidence in one's introspective evidence, the kind I pointed to earlier that comes from observing oneself as an active agent. Such self-knowledge was not enough to resist all the very heavy scientific and philosophical sophistication coming from those who championed the Newtonian picture.

FREEDOM'S COMPATIBILITY WITH NATURE

Nevertheless, that is the conclusion we now have to reach—namely, that there is, indeed, a certain irreducible element of freedom which every human being who is not suffering from major brain damage possesses. As we have noted before, that irreducible element is what in fact defines one as a person, what gives rise to the notion of human dignity.[9] Unless we divide ourselves into both a comprehensible natural part and one that is totally mysterious and beyond us—the solution proposed by Kant—we must now conclude that there is a unity between our free or self-determined and our predictable or non-self-determined nature.

9. Robert Kane, *The Significance of Free Will* (London: Oxford University Press, 1998).

As I noted earlier, the first piece of evidence available to all of us is ourselves. We can tell from just seeing how we live, what we do on almost every wakeful occasion, that a fundamental condition of our lives is to be free. Equally important is the realization that nature itself is highly varied—some things are inert, some mineral, some organic, some biological; some swim, others fly, and so on. So there is nothing odd about the presence of an entity that could exercise initiative in its life and not simply follow impulses acting upon it. In the multifacetedness of nature, free will is not an anomaly, only a novelty.

FREEDOM AND ETHICS

It is interesting that this very quickly leads to another problem, another issue that one can appreciate just by looking at one's own life. That is that this condition of fundamental freedom we face lands us in a state of enormous responsibility: It is up to us to find out what we ought to do.

Birds do not have to ask themselves, "Should I pick seeds, or should I build a nest?" Ducks do not have to wonder, "Should I fly north or south at any time?" They do what they have to. Watch any nature show, and it quickly becomes evident just how wonderfully the animal world works out, how little consternation animals experience in their lives. None need to sit around wondering "What should I do, God, I can't make up my mind here?" Not a problem. They have it made. They have the blueprint, and it's hardwired.

We human beings are not hardwired, at least as far as those actions of ours are concerned that are guided by our conceptual thinking. We have to concern ourselves about nearly everything. People have to make difficult choices in the face of all kinds of tests, as when they resist the temptations of drugs, alcohol, smoking, or other bad habits and practices or when they need to change their minds in the face of new evidence and arguments, and so forth. So we human beings constantly face the issue of choosing between alternatives, of exercising this free will responsibly, of being a moral agent, an ethical being, an ethical animal. As Mary Midgley puts it in her book, *The Ethical Primate*, we must really face up to the fact that we are not living by instinct but by choice.

That is the second answer to the question of why freedom is important. Why the fuss? Because while we have it, we are facing incredible alternatives, some of them devastating for ourselves, for those we love, for our fellow citizens. And if we do not do the right thing of our own initiative, there are devastating consequences. So another reason, then, that freedom matters is that it is extremely, intimately connected with ethics, with morality. There are no such things as guilt, regret, apology, pride, or sense of achievement if there is no free will, if there is no freedom. You cannot tell others they ought to have done better if there was no choice. It makes no sense. It amounts to nothing but wishful thinking. It is a completely misguided way, like witchcraft or demonology. Ethics would have to be a bogus enterprise in human life if freedom were not a reality. Now this does not prove freedom, but it does indicate why it is important if one is concerned about ethical matters, if one is concerned about "oughts" and "ought nots" in life.

FREEDOM AND INDIVIDUALISM

Freedom and individualism are very intimately connected. The idea that an individual matters as an individual, rather than as a member of a group or a nation or a tribe or even a family, is crucially linked to freedom. That ancient idea invoked in novels and plays and political discussions, the notion of human dignity, comes to the fore here—that we really deserve a certain kind of basic respect when our sheer potentialities are being considered. Human beings are full of such potential, and this cannot be overlooked when dealing with them properly. Even someone who is accused of the most severe crime is owed the respect due to a human being as such: Due process in the law is in part a recognition of this fact.

This, too, is intimately tied to free will. Furthermore, the notion that you can make up your mind and that you ought to be respected as a being who can not only make up his or her mind but can also use it, is indispensable to the notion of individualism. H. L. A. Hart makes the point that

> [N]o satisfactory account of what it is which makes "conduct" voluntary or involuntary, capable of covering both acts and omissions can be given in [the] terminology of "states of mind" or "mental attitude." What is required (as a minimum) is the notion of a general ability or capacity to control bodily movements, which is usually present but may be absent or impaired. . . . It is important to pause and note that if anything is "blameworthy," it is not the "state of mind" but the agent's failure to inform himself of the facts and so getting into this "state of mind."[10]

If human beings have this ability or capacity of self-control or governance, then, normally, what choices they make will guide their conduct, and this conduct can then be subject to evaluation, assessment, blame, or praise. And it is thus, in large measure, that the individual person will differentiate who he or she is from who others are, thus punctuating his or her identity as an individual. Such is the conceptual birth of political individualism, as well, wherein every individual's sovereignty is to be guarded from assault or obliteration. It is this individualism—not the artificial atomic variety that liberal individualism's critics[11] keep discussing—which is the social-political philosophy that has reached the highest of de jure realization with the founding of the American republic.

This is not to say that it was not been around before liberalism

10. H. L. A. Hart, *Punishment and Responsibility* (New York: Oxford University Press, 1968), pp. 142–43.

11. See Charles Taylor, "Atomism," in *Philosophy and the Human Sciences* (Cambridge, England: Cambridge University Press, 1985), pp. 188–210.

gained prominence in Western politics. It has been lingering there all the time. It was even there in ancient Greece. But it reached its kind of prominent emancipation only in the last 250 years. As the Nobel laureate economist Amartya Sen comments, this basic idea about human beings transcends cultural and national boundaries.[12] It is from this that the idea of human rights arises.

But the idea is faltering again in many, many places. There are people across the world, prominent people, who are once again claiming that the individual is an invention, not a discovery. The human individual, as Marx argued, was supposedly invented around the sixteenth century to serve as an ideological tool to motivate productivity. Communitarianism, the current political darling of many academic intellectuals in America, holds that an individual human being is probably only a convenient, helpful fiction. That we are really as Marx argued—perhaps in a more bellicose fashion than do some of today's socioeconomic gurus such as Amitai Etzioni and Robert Bellah—the cells of the larger organic whole of humanity or the tribe or the nation or the family or some other group. "That the human essence is the true collectivity of man,"[13] as Marx put it.

This is a very appealing pitch; after all, our community lives are crucial to us.[14] We are all extremely fond of many people around us, or at least a few, and we are linked to their lives, as well as to the lives of millions of people we do not directly know. We love them, we depend upon them, we want them, we serve them, we expect from them many good deeds, we are constantly flourishing with the aid and assistance and thoughtfulness of other human beings. We are, to some extent, social animals. Marx called us "species beings," meaning that

12. Amartya Sen, "Human Rights and Asian Values," in Tibor R. Machan, ed., *Business Ethics in the Global Market* (Stanford, Calif.: Hoover Institution Press, 1999).

13. Karl Marx, *Selected Writings*, ed. D. McLellan (London: Oxford University Press, 1977), p. 126.

14. For how that is evident in individualist thought but does not necessitate statism of any kind, see Tibor R. Machan, *Classical Individualism* (London: Routledge, 1998).

we are the only beings who truly flourish solely when the entire species does. This is wrong, but one can see its appeal because in its micro manifestation it is nearly true. Surely we can only be happy if at least those who are our intimates are flourishing as well. Yet we cannot flourish without our own reasonably successful striving, without taking and sustaining the initiative to realize our potential as the human individuals we are.

A kind of communalism is clearly part of human life—Aristotle was very good at noticing this when he discussed the nature of the polis and how human beings are by nature social animals. This is both intellectually and emotionally attractive. So it is difficult, in the face of this attractiveness, to make a serious niche for the individuality that is also essential and even more fundamental than our sociality.

But this individuality is indeed the driving motor of all the social values that we embrace, that we champion. It is because our friends, our family, our neighbors, our colleagues, our associates, our fellow human beings have things to offer that have not been there before that we value them.

I do not mean value just in the economic sense, although that is a very important part of it. Let us never demean money; it allows us to buy things, to visit friends, to travel, to go to the museum and to the theater. Let us champion economic prosperity, but partly because it is a means to ends that we champion even more. Without this individual capacity to contribute to society, to contribute to our fellow human beings and to lead and guide our own lives and enhance ourselves, the notion of society would be really quite empty. It would be like being in a large colony of people who are suffering from extreme sleepiness. It would be dull, a bit like being part of a herd of cows.

What many champions of community values fail to appreciate is that human community life is exciting and promising because it is made up of individual human beings. And their individuality is fundamentally important because they are creative agents, because they put new things into the world. They are not simply responsive, reactive beings, because they are creative and capable of initiative, their community, with its potential for wider and wider voluntary cooperation, is enormously productive and inventive, giving us all the benefits and the hazards of art, science, philosophy, religion, technology, politics, and the intricacies of human personality.

CHAPTER THREE

Making Room
for Victims

THE IMPACT OF DENYING FREEDOM

A side effect of denying free will has been the diminution of personal responsibility, guilt, culpability, blame, praise, and related elements of morality and law. We are not here talking about specific moral views, what counts as doing right and wrong, but of whether such considerations can even make sense.

The exact way in which ideas produce consequences is itself a complex issue. (I will discuss it in the last chapter of this book.) Suffice it to mention here that often people leave some of the matters that concern them to experts. Intellectuals, academicians, pundits, and such are some of the experts they trust, given that we must all economize about what, if anything, we will try to figure out fully on our own. The issue of whether we are free agents, capable of initiative, is not always complicated. When, however, experts with good credentials tell us we are being controlled by genes, DNA, history, upbringing, culture, or economic forces, with no room left for our own initiative, we will often believe and act upon the idea. One such example is how we view the power of juries. Consultants now tell us that if they get enough data on a juror, they can predict the person's verdict. This undercuts our confidence not only in other jurors but in our own independent judgment.

One of the more serious casualties of determinism is that its adoption into the culture has made the notion of the "victim" a very confusing one. This chapter addresses this point and explores some of its more important ramifications.

INITIAL CLUES

What is implicit in talking meaningfully of victims? Apart from some metaphorical uses of the concept,[1] it implies acknowledgment of human culpability or liability for certain actions. The existence of genuine victims implies culpable agents of wrongful, injurious conduct. In contrast, the concept of casualty does not imply such culpable agency—for example, cancer or earthquakes may produce casualties, whereas criminals usually act against victims.

The concept of "victim" implies recognition of responsibility for wrong conduct by some persons toward others. This recognition, in turn, suggests a particular perspective on the topic of the status of victims in any tenable social theory. It provides a clue pointing to the need to make room for personal responsibility within such a theory. Of course, there are other clues as well. The very act of theorizing or the criticism of alternative theories implies some measure of personal responsibility. As D. Bannister observed, one advancing a successful theory of human behavior "cannot present a picture of man which patently contradicts his behavior in presenting that picture."[2]

There is a radically different conception of human action, such

---

1. For example, "Gwendolyn Cafritz, Capital Hostess, 78, a Victim of Cancer," the title of a *New York Times* obituary, or the common reference to earthquake or hurricane victims.

2. D. Bannister, "Comment," in R. Borger and Frank Cioffi, eds., *Explanation in the Behavioral Sciences* (New York: Cambridge University Press, 1970), p. 417.

that its conceptualization of the human individual makes much more sense of what it is to be a victim. This basically individualist framework is committed to the real possibility of culpable moral and legal responsibility as a fact of human social life.

Yet much of contemporary social theory denies that human beings are in the last analysis individually responsible, and thus capable of being culpable, for their actions. Three examples come to mind.

First, behaviorism, which still enjoys considerable popularity within institutional psychotherapy, denies individual responsibility. As B. F. Skinner tells us, if we are to use the methods of science in the field of human affairs, we must assume that behavior is lawful and determined. We expect to discover that what a person does is the result of specifiable conditions, and that once these conditions have been discovered, we can anticipate and to some extent determine the person's actions.[3]

To avoid any possible ambiguity, we must recall Skinner's basic claim: "It appears . . . that society is responsible for the larger part of the behavior of self-control . . . but it is also behavior, and we account for it in terms of other variables in the environment and history of the individual."[4] Skinner adds, consistently, "It is these variables which provide the ultimate control."[5]

A full-blown, consistent behaviorism, then, precludes personal responsibility, and, by implication, the very existence of victims of either moral or legal wrongs, at least according to familiar ways of comprehending these ideas.

Some might hold that all that Skinner and behaviorism claim is that proper scientific methodology requires excluding certain ideas,

3. This is the essence of most forms of determinism that we have already explored in earlier chapters. The only exception is Sperry's self-determinism, wherein the individual's causal input counts as a crucial factor leading to significant conduct.

4. B. F. Skinner, *Science and Human Behavior* (New York: Macmillan, 1953), p. 6.

5. Ibid., p. 240.

for example, of criminal responsibility and of victimization. So there remains plenty of room for them outside the domain of science. Perhaps Skinner overstates his point, and when properly understood, what his behaviorism requires can be confined to the domain of experimental psychology, where it is quite useful and valid.

However, science is widely regarded as the most reliable and systematic means by which human beings are to learn about reality; so if it requires abandoning the idea of individual, personal responsibility, it is best if our ordinary understanding follows suit as early as possible. Skinner himself certainly viewed the matter along such lines. In any case, if a methodology precludes the soundness of such an idea as personal responsibility, it is difficult to know how any theory dependent on that methodology for gaining understanding could nevertheless include it.

The second example of a social theory that leaves no room for individual or personal responsibility is Marxism. Granted, it is now difficult to attribute to Marx himself any general philosophical position without some Marxist claiming that either Marx or the more developed forms of Marxism that he or she represents has been misconstrued. Nevertheless, it is safe to say that if there are any definite meanings to the words Marx wrote, we cannot escape the conclusion that he did not regard persons as individually responsible for their conduct.

It is also crucial to note that Marxism is by no means dead as social political theory or analysis. Many feminists are Marxists of one or another variety. Marxist philosophy and social theory still flourish in the academy.[6] And if this mystifies anyone, consider only that Marx himself did not regard the emergence of socialism in Russia as consistent with his own thinking.[7]

---

6. Dario Fernandez-Morera, *American Academia and the Survival of Marxist Ideas* (Westport, Conn.: Praeger, 1996).

7. Marx explained, in the preface to the Russian edition of *The Communist Manifesto*, that transforming Russia into a socialist system might be possible if Russia

For Marx, individual responsibility cannot be attributed to persons prior to the emergence of communism, wherein we would escape the necessities imposed on us by nature and precommunist society. For him, human historical development is a process closer to what we expect from the accounts of botanists, geologists, zoologists, and evolutionary biologists than to what we might receive from a historian of moral and political affairs. Marx himself made the point clearly:

> My standpoint, from which the evolution of the economic formation of society is viewed as a process of natural history, can less than any other make the individual responsible for relations whose creature he socially remains, however much he may subjectively raise himself above them.[8]

Marx gives the reason for this in his famous statement that "It is not the consciousness of men that determines their being, but, on the contrary, their social being that determines their consciousness."[9] And although Marx also declares, "it is men who change circumstances and . . . it is essential to educate the educator himself,"[10] the initiation of the change of circumstances lies with men's productive relations in society, not with their chosen (mental) conduct. This latter is considered an idealist myth in Marxism.

Just how crucial is the denial of personal responsibility in Marxism? One need only recall that virtually all of the central elements of

---

became the center of the world socialist movement and exported the revolution beyond its borders. It could also turn out that its version of socialism would produce "the socialization of poverty" because Russia never went through capitalism. See Tibor R. Machan, *Marxism: A Bourgeois Critique* (Bradford, England: MCB University Press, 1988). See also G. A. Cohen, "Marxism after the Collapse of the Soviet Union," *Journal of Ethics* 3, no. 2 (1999): 99–104.

8. Karl Marx, *Selected Writings*, ed. David McLellen (London: Oxford University Press, 1977), p. 417 (preface to volume 1 of *Das Kapital*).

9. Ibid., p. 389 (Preface to *A Critique of Political Economy*).

10. Ibid., p. 156 (third thesis on Feuerbach).

Marxian social analysis—exploitation, alienation, revolution, class consciousness—would drop out of the Marxian picture if individuals could, under normal bourgeois circumstances, determine their own actions and significantly influence their own political, economic, and social roles. Certainly, the most crucial feature of historical materialism would disappear if the inevitability of revolution were not to be understood as an inherent part of the idea of humanity's progressive development toward communism.

So Marxism, too, is a social theory that denies individual or personal responsibility, at least for human beings who are not living within a communist stage of humanity's development. Nor does Marxism leave room for some of the more sophisticated neo-Marxist claims. It will not make sense to claim that although most human beings are indeed powerless—and thus without personal responsibility for what happens to them in life—members of the ruling class (for example, capitalists and corporate managers) are indeed culpable. It makes no sense at all that they are personally responsible, for example, for perpetuating social structures that thwart social progress.

This kind of Marxian analysis would imply holding reactionaries responsible for their victimization of the working classes. Yet, for Marxism to be the interesting, exciting, and most of all distinctive social theory that it has been taken to be, the movement of human development along dialectical lines cannot be a matter of personal choice, neither at the level of analysis nor practice nor even at the level of the ruling class.

The prominence of Marxian analysis is undeniable, despite some serious misgivings about Marxism by many of its contemporary champions. And the logic of Marxism, as well as of neo-Marxism, denies that individuals are responsible for what they do. So from within Marxism, too, no room can be found for the concept of a victim in social or legal theory. Indeed, it is arguable that this explains in large part why so much brutality could be performed in the name of Marxism, never mind whether Marx himself would have been for or against it.

The third example of a deterministic perspective that has gained prominence in our time is sociobiology[11] or neo-Darwinism.[12] There is no room for the concept of "individual or personal responsibility" and thus for victimization in this viewpoint. If it is ultimately our genes or natural selection that propels us to behave the way we do, surely it is nonsense to hold individuals responsible for what they do to others, be it beneficial or harmful. Take a less widely known version of the socio-biological perspective, in which the earth itself "is most like a single cell." So, "[w]e should credit [the earth] for what it is: for sheer size and perfection of function, it is far and away the grandest product of collaboration in all of nature."[13] Once again, individual responsibility for what happens on earth, all the way from ecological misconduct to crime, must be precluded in such a position. Ordinarily no one would think of blaming or crediting a person's separate fingers, joints, or-gans, or limbs for any crucial behavior or its consequences. So if the globe really is like a cell—that is, an organism of which we human beings are merely parts, segments, or portions—then we are no more responsible for what happens than are our body parts, even in cases of the most viciously calculated victimization.

There are a few prominent views that dissent from the aforemen-tioned, but even they do not hold out much promise for the concept of individual moral or legal responsibility and, thus, for the concept of a victim in social theory. Although existentialism, for example, does admit that some measure of human freedom of choice exists, it never-theless denies that there is an objective standard of conduct for eval-uating the acts that human beings admittedly, by existentialist theory, choose to perform. So freedom of choice is affirmed here, but any idea

11. See Edward O. Wilson, *Sociobiology: The New Synthesis* (Cambridge, Mass.: Harvard University Press, 1984).

12. Richard Dawkins, *The Selfish Gene* (London: Oxford University Press, 1976). But see also, Steven Rose, *Lifelines: Biology beyond Determinism* (London: Oxford University Press, 1997).

13. Lewis Thomas, *The Lives of a Cell* (New York: Viking, 1974), p. 4.

of right and wrong is banished (at least at a fundamental level of this perspective).[14] For there to be victims, something wrong must have been done to someone by someone else. Yet, if no standard of right and wrong exists, then there is no basis for claiming that something wrong is ever done to anyone, even when that something is harmful and was done to someone by another as a matter of free choice. From such a state of affairs no coherent social theory of victimization can emerge. Nor need we confine ourselves to existentialism when we observe the denial of objective standards of right and wrong in contemporary views of human life. The bulk of contemporary philosophical ethics and, consequently, jurisprudence denies the possibility of objective standards of right and wrong, even while condemning the immorality of egoism or hedonism (from heaven knows what basis!).[15]

We can then fairly assert that much of contemporary social theory leaves no room for individual or personal moral and legal responsibility, either because it denies basic choice to individuals or because it denies any basis of an objective differentiation between right and wrong conduct.

There can be little dispute about the fact that, in positive law, ideas carry considerable impact. After all, in legislatures, in courts, and in political theory people put forth arguments that often lead to convictions and are translated into legal norms. Most recently, for example, the views of several legal theorists have made an impact on Anglo-American jurisprudence. Ronald Dworkin has spearheaded the reconsideration of a somewhat perplexing version of natural law theory.[16] Not only does Dworkin argue that there exists some basis for

14. For one of the best expositions of this existentialist stance, see Hazel Barnes, *An Existentialist Ethics* (New York: Random House, 1967).

15. A prominent example, by now a sort of contemporary classic, is Bernard Williams, *Ethics and the Limits of Philosophy* (Cambridge, Mass.: Harvard University Press, 1985).

16. Ronald Dworkin, *Taking Rights Seriously* (Cambridge, Mass.: Harvard University Press, 1977).

objective moral truth, but he also advances many substantive theses as to what decisions courts should make in various kinds of cases, decisions he believes are justified by certain fundamental and objective moral principles.

From a different viewpoint there has emerged another influential idea, namely, the economic analysis of the law, developed by such legal theorists as Richard Posner.[17] Here the stress is placed not on some alleged objective basis for moral and legal judgments but on the idea that law ultimately reflects the principles of economic efficiency. In effect, the "law and economics" thesis holds that from common law all the way to the decisions of high courts, rulings tend on the whole to reflect what will in fact yield the most economical arrangements within a given human community. Although the substance of this view would pretty much diminish if not eliminate the role of individual responsibility in human affairs—because it assumes the inevitable force of economic efficiency as the prime motivator of human behavior—there is no doubt that the theory itself has had considerable impact. (Posner himself is now on the bench!)

What is interesting about these influential views of the nature of law is that in certain respects they embrace notions that are deemed alien to them. First, Dworkin, although he has rekindled an interest in moral principles and, thus, in personal moral and legal responsibility, is in fact a political egalitarian and finds the idea of the right to individual liberty unfounded. Yet that idea is central to the belief in individual moral responsibility. If one is not free to act as one chooses—if the law compels one to do the right thing, if political regulation instead of individual conscience determines how members of a human community will conduct themselves—then one cannot be morally responsible for what one does. This view, then, is plagued by the opposite problem from the one we identified in connection with existentialism. To endorse moral responsibility without the right to

17. Richard Posner, *The Economic Analysis of Law* (Boston: Little, Brown, 1972).

individual liberty is no better than to endorse human liberty but deny moral standards by which this liberty ought to be exercised.

On the other hand, the perspective embraced by Posner and his followers favors a more or less unregulated economic and social system, one that leaves matters of economic and cultural development to individuals. Thus this view is often considered to be conservative and even libertarian, favoring, as it seems, individual liberty over social regulation. Yet since the view also accepts the *homo economicus* conception of human nature, whereby individuals are automatic utility maximizers, it rules out individual responsibility.

So here too we see that contemporary currents of thought undercut the basis for a cogent idea of victimization, either by endorsing large-scale social engineering (à la Dworkin's egalitarianism) or by relying on the idea of built-in motivations to explain human behavior (à la Posner's economic-man idea). Is there any viewpoint that may serve as an alternative to those mentioned above, which clearly leave no cogent place for the concept of the victim in social theory? In the following section I discuss such an alternative and some of its advantages from the point of view of social theory. This is far from an exhaustive development, but it should at least offer some initial steps in a very possibly fruitful direction.

THE CRIMINAL AND THE VICTIM

The notion that there are human victims presupposes certain factors. And the absence of these factors belies the concept of "victim" in the first place, just as a viewpoint that precludes magic simply cannot make sense of the concept of "witch" and just as a secular scientific framework has no place for such an entity as the "devil."

In turn, a social theory in which individuals are only parts of the whole organism of humanity (or society or race or species) precludes the concept "victim." Take what we ordinarily regard to be an individual person as an example. If in the course of our lives one of us would find it necessary to harm some limb, we would not regard this as a case of victimization. When the Irish actor Richard Harris had his nose rebuilt using bone extracted from his pelvis, nobody could reasonably construe his pelvis as a victim, except perhaps metaphorically. Similarly, when we subject ourselves to severe stress in an effort to achieve some important goal—for example, to climb the Matterhorn—it makes no sense to regard this as victimizing our body or nerves or whatever else may suffer in the process. In general, it is not sensible to regard persons who are assaulted or harmed by others against their will as parts of some whole that must sometimes be harmed for the benefit of the whole. Of course, it might be argued that we are wrong to treat persons differently, but what can this mean other than that we should not so regard persons? That, however, assumes that we have a choice about how we regard people, whether we are going to regard them as responsible individuals or as parts of wholes that are expendable when the need arises. But that, in turn, assumes that we have a choice and are individually responsible for making the right one.

All in all, then, the ordinary view seems philosophically reasonable enough. But it is also clear that this perspective is not widely defended. Even those who would seem to favor it tend to embrace ideas that contradict it. I have already mentioned the "law and economics" school. Other conservative viewpoints, more closely aligned with traditional theism, would tend also to make individuals parts of some greater whole—or at least dependent on some higher reality to which they owe their identity and loyalty. Nevertheless, there exists an implicit individualism in our criminal law, whereby individuals are often regarded as morally and legally culpable and are not expendable even for the sake of attaining very noble goals. This view has some theoretical support from existing philosophical perspectives, even if these have not reached the kind of prominence required for them to become the foundation of social theorizing.[18]

In particular, the idea is present within the Anglo-American political tradition that individuals possess basic rights, namely, to life, liberty, and the pursuit of happiness. If these rights are well founded, they testify to something of a philosophical base for individualism. But this individualism is not the kind that is most often discussed, namely, the kind we associate with the philosophy of Thomas Hobbes, whereby an individual human being possesses its individuality, as do many other objects, only in being separate from others in time and space.[19] Rather, the individual presupposed in the Lockean doctrine of rights is a human individual. That is to say, he or she is not an atomic self, entirely unique and merely conventionally human. Rather he or she is an individual of a certain kind, but by being a certain kind of individual he or she does not become deprived of individuality, as in such collectivist outlooks as Marxism. Being a human being within this individualist perspective means that it is most rational to classify someone as having natural similarities with others, as being a natural kind, but not as being part of a larger individual—for example, the entity called humanity.

With this individualism we must also find a theory of free action before we can cogently discuss individual or personal moral and legal responsibility. But that requires some cogent idea of self-determination. The doctrine of free will must be recaptured in such a form that

18. A while ago A. R. Louch, in *Explanation and Human Action* (Berkeley: University of California Press, 1969), and H. Harre and P. F. Secord, in *The Explanation of Social Behavior* (Totowa, N.J.: Littlefield, Adams and Co., 1973), gave support to it. Now it is Edward Pols, in *The Acts of Our Being* (Amherst: University of Massachusetts Press, 1982), who argues it forcefully.

19. The contrast between this quantitative and a qualitative individualism is discussed in David L. Norton, *Personal Destinies: A Philosophy of Ethical Individualism* (Princeton, N.J.: Princeton University Press, 1976). See also Tibor R. Machan, *Capitalism and Individualism: Reframing the Argument for the Free Society* (New York: St. Martin's Press, 1990).

it does not fly in the face of the findings of science. And indeed there is reason to believe that this is a promising prospect. Contrary to Skinner, for example, it is not a requirement of science that behavior be always linked to some prior sufficient cause. Rather, as I noted in chapter 1, Sperry and others have argued that it is possible to construe the highly developed human organism as making it possible for individual human beings to engage in (self-)initiated conduct.[20] This is a variety of causality in the universe, not some contradiction to or escape from causality, as critics of the free-will position have often alleged.

Although the last several centuries of mechanistic scientism would dismiss this idea, there is no such easy way to do so within the framework of a nonreductionist conception of causality and the nature of reality, one that is gaining better footing in our time.[21] But where does this lead us vis-à-vis the other problem—namely, whether any basis of moral and legal responsibility is available, and whether objective moral and legal norms can be identified?

Here is where the fact that this individualist viewpoint does not derive its philosophical basis from Hobbes comes to be significant. Since we are considering human individuals, the proper conduct, the moral life, of each individual must first of all do full justice to one's humanity. There are universal standards, albeit few, implicit in this fact. Yet since the human essence, contrary to Marx, is not "the true collectivity of man" but rather the true individuality of man,[22] neither

20. Roger W. Sperry, "Changing Concepts of Consciousness and Free Will," *Perspectives in Biology and Medicine* 9 (August 1976): 9–19.

21. For a discussion of this, see Pols, *The Acts of Our Being*. See also Tibor R. Machan, *The Pseudo-science of B. F. Skinner* (New Rochelle, N.Y.: Arlington House Publishing Co., 1974).

22. I develop this idea at length in Tibor R. Machan, *Classical Individualism: The Supreme Importance of Each Human Being* (London: Routledge, 1998). Marx and even his less doctrinaire followers (e.g., Charles Taylor) laid out a collectivist conception of human beings. The idea that "the human essence is the true collectivity of man" fails to appreciate the creative nature of every human individual, something I call attention to in this book and have done elsewhere.

is it possible in morality to ignore individual differences. Whereas universality may be possible for only some very general moral principles, objectivity could be possible for any moral judgment. This is because the individual human being is an objective fact, and what will make that individual's life an excellent one is dependent on what and who that particular individual is. All this is identifiable, although the process is not simple and the results not preordained.

All of the above is but the beginning of a philosophical individualism that makes it possible to construe human beings as individuals who have moral and legal responsibilities. It is, then, also possible to consider that such individuals can be agents of wrong acts. Some of these acts may be directed against other individuals, who then would be the victims of the former—that is, the victims of culpable violators of the rights of the person they have wrongfully injured or harmed or otherwise intruded upon.

This is certainly only the broadest outline for a social theory within which victimization makes cogent sense. But all in all even at this abstract level one can see that the position accords with much of our common sense, jurisprudential tradition, and personal practice as theorists concerned with the questions that give rise to the position itself.

We see here a sketch of a position that makes room for the idea that we ourselves are responsible, professionally, for the quality of the theories we propose. Other positions we have considered cannot make the same claim.

The position also makes room for the admittedly loosely grasped and somewhat confused but firmly held view that sometimes human beings do wrong to others and that sometimes they are personally to be blamed for this. As members of an organized human community, as citizens, we also see that the position allows that some of those who are wronged by others are properly regarded as victims, whereas those who did the victimization are culpable for what they did and may have to be treated accordingly.

If the above idea can also enjoy philosophical and scientific support, as I have suggested, then perhaps we can take comfort in what one of the few contemporary theorists of individualism has observed:

> Beneath the accretions of contravening epochs and cultures a vestige of the original eudaimonistic intuition endures today, I believe, in the individual's residual conviction of his own irreplaceable worth. But this small conviction is wholly unequipped to withstand the drubbing it takes from the world, and from which all too often it never recovers. At its first appearance it is buffeted by alarms and commotion, and trampled beneath the scurrying crowd. Propped upright it is conscripted to this cause or that where roll call is "by the numbers," truth is prescribed, and responsibility is collective, the individual's share being determined by arithmetic apportionment. What remains is a merely numerical individuation, deriving its fugitive worth from the collective whole of which it is a replaceable part.[23]

VICTIMS MAY BE CHAMPIONS

If the individualism I have been mentioning here allows for victims, it also allows for those who would resist victimization, those who would choose to strive for justice in the face of it. So there is much more to the position than its allowing for the concept of "victim." It also makes it possible to think of righting the wrong of victimization. If the position is sound, it follows that human beings are both subject to victimization and able to forge responses, personal and institutional, to this fact of their existence. It follows, in short, that the idea of bona fide victimization is itself more potent than those theories that deny victimization and can only make room for casualties of the forces of impersonal nature.[24]

23. Norton, *Personal Destinies*, p. x.
24. I say "casualties" because that is how we designate those who suffer the more severe consequences of natural mishaps or "acts of God," such as earthquakes, viral epidemics, and so forth.

Social theory may, of course, have to admit that it cannot confine itself to a value-free stance if there is room in it for personal moral and legal responsibility. Social theorists themselves may have to alter their way of acting, perhaps by championing the cause of a certain kind of ontological individualism. This would give them theoretical ground for the influence that they have, not surprisingly, tried to muster. But there should be no a priori resistance to that fact. It would simply bring to the fore something that has been in the background all along, namely, that social theory is essentially normative.

CHAPTER FOUR

Two Ways to Liberalism

TWO TYPES OF LIBERALISM

Let me begin with some observations at a very abstract level concerning some unavoidable features of human life and the world in which it plays itself out. I think that no attempt to clarify these can get far without taking into account the fact of human initiative. This is not unlike trying to make sense of art without recourse to the fact of human imagination.

We all can appreciate the fact that reality is nuanced, often with minute variations that confound us in all realms, including biology, zoology, botany, and all spheres in which human intelligence has had great influence. Furthermore, apart from the objective presence of complexities and diversities in our ways of living, there are also the much more diverse conceptions of how we might and ought to configure our lives. Adding, then, to nature's diversity are the results of human beings' efforts to conceptualize nature, including their place in it, more or less accurately. Put plainly, we face not just nature's diversity but the diversity of our thinking about nature, something that also produces lasting variations in how we live. As a result, there are objectively warranted variations in how human beings ought to organize their communities—in view of diverse requirements they face at different times and in different places—aside from simple accidental differences and those that are produced by subjective factors such as tastes and preferences.

This immense and complex fact-based diversity and the far more than corresponding diversity in our perspectives are best explained by taking account of human initiative, among other matters, in how we understand humankind. If we had no choice about how to view the world, we would certainly have fewer worldviews competing for acceptance.

Not surprisingly, we also create innumerable types of political orders and many variations within them (represented by diverse renditions of, for example, anarchism, statism, socialism, capitalism, and other conceptions of social organization). If we add to this our proclivity as theorists to put even well-traveled matters a bit idiosyncratically, we will quickly appreciate why we abound in variations on all themes that catch our attention.[1]

Furthermore, over time the way we understand reality changes, too, because of the opportunities we may have exploited to be better informed, to organize our concepts more sharply, and to take into account newly discovered differences and similarities. Thus even a basically sound understanding of some feature of reality is likely to undergo alterations, modifications, and revisions.

This is also true of classical liberalism, or what has come in our

1. Why does this not appear to be true in the formal and the natural sciences, such as logic and chemistry? Partly because the subject matter is more simple and general—one studies electrons not as individuals or even special collections but simply as electrons. And a logical inference, just in terms of being what it is, is independent of any variations of content or substance. Beginning with the biological sciences, however, not to mention the humanities, variation is the ontological norm. Individual and special differences become vital. Furthermore, there are personal and special goals that begin to be served in how an account of such matters is laid out, what is stressed, and so forth. None of this makes the substance of the discussion in these areas ontologically any less concrete and definite.

time to be called libertarianism, the polity that rests, in part, on the belief in the essential place of human initiative in our lives and the primary significance of making room for its exercise in human communities. It will be worth our time to examine the ways this political order has been supported in the past and what kind of support for it may be the most successful.

For those in the West, especially the United States, the various ways of understanding liberalism can be rather frustrating, even annoying, since the term "liberty" has had not just analytic but a good deal of normative, even emotive significance. So how we use the term is going to matter to many people and call forth considerable skepticism, even rebuke, from those who have a different definition to offer.

It is utopian to believe that perfect identity of meaning will ever be attained on any term. This is especially true of terms that carry normative implications, since each of us has a stake in getting our idiosyncratic ways recorded just so. However, it borders on corruption to try to win one's ethical or political disputes by perpetrating blatant conceptual revisions. For example, "liberalism" in popular political parlance has come to mean, at least in the United States, the championing of a strong welfare state. Why call this "liberalism" when in its original political usage the term suggested ideas and ideals very different from what the welfare state stresses—such as limited government and the right to personal liberty and to private property?

One might argue that there had been some kind of sleight of hand at play here, and, no doubt, this suspicion is quite plausible. The same is true about the kin concept "rights" when it is used to claim that we all have a basic right to welfare, health care, and so forth. How can that be, when this means that others must produce those for us, thus requiring a system of involuntary servitude? The concept "democracy" is similarly subject to case-pleading revisions—regimes are deemed democratic by virtue of their alleged concern for all, never mind that only a few have a hand in governance.

Political mileage can be gained from persuading many people, ones who do not practice independent thinking on such matters, to pick up on the implications of such revisionist political linguistics. Thus "freedom" or "liberty" can soon be used to mean just the opposite, namely, involuntary servitude. "Rights," too, will come to mean legally enforceable obligations, not liberty as in freedom from other people's intrusive conduct upon oneself.

Yes, there is a good deal of subterfuge about concepts like these, ones Alasdair MacIntyre once dubbed "essentially contestable." Nevertheless, there are some mitigating factors that also produce such complexity of meaning and use.

For example, one can find a respectable enough tradition in Western political thought that supports the current use of "liberal" in American politics. Socialists have clearly embraced what has come to be called the idea of positive freedom, from which this current use arises.[2] It is used to mean "the condition of being enabled to reach a desired or desirable goal," as in "the truth shall set you free."

When one is free of disease, free of ignorance, free of poverty, one is free in this sense. Furthermore, once the idea of self-causation, self-determination, origination, or personal initiative is left philosophically unsupported—apparently even scientifically hopeless—the sense of being free as meaning that no one intrudes upon one or aggresses against someone carries little significance. Marx characterized it as mere bourgeois freedom compared with true human freedom.

Aggression from others under such conditions is but a natural impediment, no different from the "aggression" that a tornado or virus will manifest. The only true freedom is what Marx advanced, following Hegel: freedom from natural necessity. And the only way he saw that we might achieve it is to patiently await the time when history ushers it into our lives. Yet other socialists did not abide by such patience and thus developed the political movement that embraces positive

---

2. Tom Campbell, *The Left and Rights: A Conceptual Analysis of the Idea of Socialist Rights* (London: Routledge and Kegan Paul, 1983).

freedom and positive rights, which have public policy implications that are virtually diametrically opposed to those of negative freedom or rights.[3]

That human beings are most in need of this kind of "freedom of impediments" is a notion some neoclassical economists, such as the late George Stigler, also embraced. Accordingly, freedom is really nothing more than wealth or diminished cost, the reduction of obstacles to overcome in one's life.[4]

Actually, classical liberalism, which has had certain affinities with modern scientism, has unwittingly accepted an understanding of human nature in terms of which we are passive, inert, and incapable of self-determination, the very idea that has spawned philosophical support for the welfare state. In other words, one of the paths to classical liberalism can lead, as well, to contemporary welfare statism. In that outlook, after all, it is central that people are taken to be victims—or, rather, casualties—of their circumstances deserving neither credit nor blame for their lot in life.[5]

It is, however, contemporary liberalism—as associated with the views of American democrats, the Americans for Democratic Action, the editorialists of the *New York Times*, and so forth—that is most clearly loyal to positive freedom. It arises from the understanding of

3. For more on this, see Tibor R. Machan, "The Nonexistence of Basic Welfare Rights," in James Sterba, ed., *Justice: Alternative Political Perspectives* (Belmont, Calif.: Wadsworth Publishing Co., 1992), which is a chapter from Tibor R. Machan, *Individuals and Their Rights* (LaSalle, Ill.: Open Court Publishing Co., 1989).

4. Welfare-statists—such as John Rawls in his *A Theory of Justice* (Cambridge, Mass.: Harvard University Press, 1971)—go on to argue that since no one is more deserving of success than another, since everything just happens, nothing is ultimately up to any of us; in a just society everyone ought to have as much of everything good for us as is possible to arrange via effective, collective, state action. That, too, leads to a polity in which basic positive freedom is prized above everything else.

5. See chapter 3. The idea is that since human beings, as everything else, are subject to the Newtonian laws of physics, they cannot be expected to help themselves out of dire straits but must rely on the powerful, forceful state to enable them to improve their lives.

human nature as basically inert, as all of matter happens to be in the framework of the ontology of classical mechanics. So what people need is not to be left free by their fellows but to be made free by enabling them to overcome natural impediments to their motion and development. And thus government ought to free them from their hardship. (How "ought" claims can fit this framework is, of course, a very serious and unsolved puzzle.)

Actually, neither classical nor modern liberalism is spared scorn from some of our major political philosophers. MacIntyre, for example, heaps such scorn on liberalism in great abundance:

> [T]he Marxist understanding of liberalism as ideological, as a deceiving and self-deceiving mask for certain social interests, remains compelling. . . . Liberalism in the name of freedom imposes a certain kind of unacknowledged domination, and one which in the long run tends to dissolve traditional human ties and to impoverish social and cultural relationships. Liberalism, while imposing through state power regimes that declare everyone free to pursue whatever they take to be their own good, deprives most people of the possibility of understanding their lives as a quest for the discovery and achievement of the good, especially by the way in which it attempts to discredit those traditional forms of human community within which this project has to be embodied.[6]

In other words, classical liberalism is a ruse, a system that pretends to serve justice but, in fact, serves special interests while destroying the conditions for a decent life among ordinary people. Marx put the matter even more directly:

> This kind of liberty [free competition] is thus at the same time the most complete suppression of all individual liberty and total subjugation of individuality to social conditions which take the form of

---

6. Alasdair MacIntyre, "Nietzsche or Aristotle?" in Giovanna Borradori, *The American Philosopher* (Chicago: University of Chicago Press, 1994), p. 143.

material forces—and even of all-powerful objects that are independent of the individuals relating to them. The only rational answer to the deification of free competition by the middle-class prophets, or its diapolisation by the socialists, lies in its own development.[7]

The usual tirades against at least classical liberalism—that it fosters atomism and subjective autonomy and thus ethical relativism, decadence, and social life that rests on power rather than right—may all be added to this lament. It is voiced by conservatives as well as radicals, by some Christians as well as most communitarians.[8] It is the refrain we hear from such diverse sources as the crude talk shows and erudite commentaries by famous academics.

Is there anything to these vehement sentiments or are they yet another example of sophisticated ranting and raving about a system that simply will not allow intellectuals to have much more say about systems of governance than ordinary people who like to eat at McDonalds, be entertained via MTV, and shop at Wal-Mart? In short, are all these complaints sour grapes?

The honest answer is that, if only inadvertently, MacIntyre's and Marx's hostility has something, albeit minimal, going for it. The lamentable features of liberalism have to do with failing to distinguish two considerably different ways in which the system can be defended and insisting on advancing one as superior to the other, whereas probably just the opposite is the case.

Putting it plainly, denying that liberalism has a normative dimension, that it tells not what is the case but also what should be done, will not wash, and critics of the system are aware of this, so they label defenders who rest on such a scientistic argument frauds. This may be wrong as far as what is being intended is concerned, but it may hint at something deceptive, if unintentionally so. The effort to promote a

---

7. Karl Marx, *Grundrisse* (New York: Harper and Row, 1970), p. 131.

8. Amitai Etzioni, Charles Taylor, Roger Scruton, and others have voiced such laments.

system of political economy cannot escape a normative component, and to believe it can is self-deceptive.

TWO CLASSICAL LIBERAL TRADITIONS

The case for a free society, as understood within the earlier classical liberal traditions, has been advanced on several bases. These include skepticism, mysticism, positivism, natural law and natural rights, utilitarianism, and pragmatism. In its infancy and adolescence, liberalism was primarily defended as a modern approach to politics that has gained much of its strength from certain affinities with science. The earlier and later prominent defenses may be broadly distinguished as the positive and the normative cases for freedom.

It was the twentieth-century novelist-philosopher Ayn Rand who put on record the most fully developed—though insufficiently detailed—normative argument for classical liberal ideas and ideals, ones that dominate the discussion of the merits and liabilities of classical liberalism in our day. Earlier hints of such a defense were available from John Locke and others in the natural-law school of moral and political philosophy. In our time, it has been Robert Nozick, Loren Lomasky, Douglas B. Rasmussen and Douglas J. Den Uyl, Fred D. Miller Jr., and I who have carried forth this normative tradition.

In contrast, the most persistent contemporary positive case in economics has been advanced by Milton Friedman. He has given a direct treatment of certain methodological issues that serves as the philosophical foundation of such an approach to social philosophy. Some others in that field of positive political economy—for example, David Friedman, George Stigler (now deceased), and Gary Becker, both Nobel laureates—have also contributed to this nonnormative approach to political economy. The late Ludwig von Mises and F. A. Hayek are among them, as are the philosophers Jan Narveson and David Conway.[9]

In the classical liberal tradition—as in many other schools, including socialism—there has always been this division between the positive (or "scientific") versus the normative (or "ethical") defenses of the free society with, of course, some shadings in between that are difficult to classify. Yet in the earlier incarnations of the position, the positivist stance was clearly dominant.

The nonnormative case can be traced, philosophically, to Thomas Hobbes, as well as Baruch Spinoza, and includes such classical champions of economic liberty as Adam Smith, John Stuart Mill, and David Ricardo. Positivists today are still better positioned academically, but their approach is no longer so widely championed. A few years ago one could encounter Milton Friedman and F. A. Hayek on *Meet the Press* and read Friedman regularly in *Newsweek* magazine. Friedman still appears on the editorial page of the *Wall Street Journal* now and again. You can see the same prominence, for example, evident in the appointment of Richard Posner as judge of the Seventh District Court

9. Although John Locke's liberalism is usually classified as a normative approach, Locke himself seemed inconsistent in his approach to philosophy in general as well as to political theory. In the former he was, like Thomas Hobbes, a materialist and empiricist. (It was some of the theological approaches that would best qualify as normative defenses—e.g., advanced by Francisco Suarez, Samuel Puffendorf, and M. J. de Condorcet.) In our own day the examples of the positivist approach in political philosophy are Jan Narveson, *The Libertarian Idea* (Philadelphia, Pa.: Temple University Press, 1988) and David Conway, *Classical Liberalism* (London: Macmillan Press, 1995), and, of course, many more in formal economics and political economy (Milton Friedman, George Stigler, Gordon Tullock, et al.). The normative approach is exemplified now in the works of Loren Lomasky, *Persons, Rights, and the Moral Community* (London: Oxford University Press, 1987), Douglas B. Rasmussen and Douglas J. Den Uyl, *Liberty and Nature: An Aristotelian Defense of Liberal Order* (LaSalle, Ill.: Open Court Publishing Co., 1991), as well as myself and others who carry on the work of the novelist-philosopher Ayn Rand. (I will address Hayek's efforts in the next chapter of this book.)

in Chicago, as well as by the number of Nobel Prizes received by other scientific economists who defend a free-market system of economic arrangements for human communities. The books of these social scientist champions of classical liberalism are very well published by prominent publishers such as the University of Chicago, Harvard University, University of California, and other premier presses. We will shortly get to those who advance the moral defense, one that today seems to be more widely championed, especially in the circles of scholars who discuss political theory and philosophy. In other words, if we take John Rawls as the philosophical representative of the social democratic—or modern liberal—welfare state, it is Nozick, Lomasky, Rasmussen and Den Uyl, and some others who are discussed at times as the classical liberal or libertarian counterpoints.

LIBERALISM'S EARLIER LOVE AFFAIR WITH SCIENCE

There is little doubt that the social scientific defense of freedom once had a better standing than the moral defense in the community of political inquirers. This is because the normative defense has seemed weak and flawed in light of the scientism of the last several centuries. Many thinkers were thoroughly convinced of the arationality of normative discourse following David Hume's assertion that no "ought" claims can be deduced from "is" claims. A great deal of respect had also been accorded to approaching a problem along lines similar to those spelled out in the natural sciences for reasons that are not difficult to appreciate. They promise rigor, exactitude, precision, and practical usefulness. They also suggested that complex human problems—psychological, ethical, political, and so forth—could be dealt with in the proven ways of technology.

The modern era's confidence in what B. F. Skinner called "the technology of culture" can be appreciated once one considers the rapid progress of the natural sciences and the resulting technological advances, along with the age-old propensity of intellectuals to seek for unifying systems of thought so as to make sense of reality. The persistent hope for the Archimedian point from which all problems could be solved with adequate information at hand has sometimes led philosophers of the highest quality to jump to hasty generalizations when they were inspired and excited enough about how we might go about solving pressing human problems.[10]

For the last four hundred years in Western civilization, the scientific mode of thinking has proven impressive, if only by way of its great contribution to productivity. It still is, of course, although much dismay is now evident with extrapolating the methods of the natural sciences to all other studies. Most of our technology, productivity, the gadgets we now take for granted are linked to science, and among many this still sustains a confidence in applying universally the sort of thinking that seems to have made them possible. The hopefulness in social engineering can be accounted for by reference to the prevalence of scientific thinking, even scientism. Except for Immanuel Kant, few have attempted to abandon scientism wholesale, and Kant did it at the cost of reinvigorating dualism, which has always been intellectually uncomfortable to accept because, among other reasons, of the problem of interactionism.

Another important reason why the positivist approach had been widely embraced is that the only powerful normative defense of liberalism had purged prudence from its midst. Kantianism, though normative and supportive of classical liberal institutions, had no solid place for the prime candidate that might have been used to defend the classical liberal economic order on moral grounds, namely, for the moral virtue of prudence.

Within this tradition of ethical thinking, goals or results—that is, the ends or objectives of action—and the virtues enabling one to reach

10. I discuss this as the "blow-up fallacy" in *The Pseudo-Science of B. F. Skinner* (New Rochelle, N.Y.: Arlington House Publishing Co., 1973).

them are deemed to be morally irrelevant. Doing what is right cannot be defended by reference to one's ends, only by reference to the dictates of a categorical imperative.

Yet, if prudence—which aims at self-enhancement—is not a virtue, it is difficult to see how one could morally respect the activities that make up much of the free market. There can be nothing seriously right about striving to make a profit, trying to prosper in life.[11] Virtues such as frugality, industry, fortitude, and such are unavailable as bona fide moral traits within the post-Kantian moral philosophical tradition.

Yes, some defenders of liberalism appear to find it sufficient, from the moral point of view, that in a liberal polity all interpersonal actions are done by mutual consent. Yet this is not sufficient, because people can cooperate to their own moral detriment—for example, when they exchange heroin for cocaine and both proceed to abuse the drugs. Freedom is not really a personal virtue but a precondition of such virtues. As Hayek (paradoxically, considering his preference for the nonnormative approach) wrote: "That freedom is the matrix required for the growth of moral values—indeed not merely one value among many but the source of all values—is almost self-evident. It is only where the individual has choice, and its inherent responsibility, that he has occasion to affirm existing values, to contribute to their further growth, and then earn moral merit."[12]

Freedom is a precondition of personal virtue, of doing the morally right thing, rather than itself such a virtue. And unless the liberal capitalist society can also claim for itself the achievement of fostering personal virtues, it will lack moral standing. The prominent older

11. For an extensive development of this idea, see James E. Chesher and Tibor R. Machan, *The Business of Commerce: Examining an Honorable Profession* (Stanford, Calif.: Hoover Institution Press, 1999).

12. F. A. Hayek, "The Moral Element in Free Enterprise," in Mark W. Hendrickson, ed., *The Morality of Capitalism* (Irvington-on-Hudson, N.Y.: Foundation for Economic Education, 1992). This is actually a curious remark from Hayek, who tended to eschew moral arguments. Yet it is sound, nevertheless.

versions of classical liberalism, therefore, rested mainly on nonmoral defenses of the system.

So the main reason for the superior reputation of the positivist approach is that many people have had great confidence in science, and the only prominent moral framework offered no support for liberal (bourgeois) virtues. Even in our time, when popular discourse is filled with references to ethics, family values, the cowardice of terrorists, and so forth, many academic intellectuals who support classical liberal ideals would not defend the position that there are objective moral or ethical truths. The primary stance on such topics is well voiced by Richard Rorty when he says that "Non-metaphysicians [of whom Rorty and, by his account, all other wise men are members] cannot say that democratic institutions reflect a moral reality and that tyrannical regimes do not reflect one, that tyrannies get something wrong that democratic societies get right."[13]

Although Rorty himself is of the communitarian Left today, certain noted classical liberals, such as Richard Posner, have embraced his philosophical stance as supportive of the free society.[14] And if we include among liberals the left-leaning welfare-statists who do not quite wish to give up on some of liberalism's key ideas—for example, John Rawls—it is not difficult to see that their meager normative framework is closer to positivism than many realize. Rawls, for example, champions the intuitionist approach to ethics, and in the last analysis, by denying any significant role to free will, has no room for praise and blame within his moral framework.[15]

13. Richard Rorty, "The Seer of Prague," *New Republic* (July 1, 1991): 35–40.

14. Richard Posner, *Pragmatism versus the Rule of Law* (Washington, D.C.: American Enterprise Institute, 1991 [transcript of lecture]).

15. See John Rawls, *A Theory of Justice* (Cambridge, Mass.: Harvard University Press, 1971), p. 104, where he claims that "The assertion that a man deserves the superior character that enables him to make the effort to cultivate his abilities is . . . problematic; for his character depends in large part upon fortunate family and social circumstances for which he can claim no credit." Although this does not quite embrace

This means that some of the very prominent defenders of the free society, whether in its pure libertarian or watered down welfare-statist version, have been and still are skeptical of making a moral case for their system. The exception is an intuitive, subjective basis, one that clearly has no other implication than that the proponent prefers something that he calls good or right.

Those in the classical liberal or libertarian orbit have in the past mainly thought, basically, that when a society enjoys minimal obstruction to the movement human beings are naturally inclined to make forward, to pursue their utility or happiness, this will amount to the most suitable social state for them—ergo, noninterventionist government, laissez-faire, civil liberties, and so forth. The case for liberty has been and still is often made, therefore, without reference to the troublesome, mythical area of values, norms, or morals. These do not measure up to the requirements of scientism, the ontology of mechanics.

MORALITY'S PHILOSOPHICAL DEMISE

Thus, for several centuries, morality or ethics had been unseated from its prominence as part of humanistic studies. From ancient Greece up until the Middle Ages, morality had been taken seriously, albeit often, especially in popular circles, as a means to prepare people for the afterlife. To wit, the notion that human beings are the sort of creatures who can make choices between right and wrong, that they have the responsibility to do the right thing, and that when they do wrong, they are blameworthy for this—this view had been very prominent in Augustine, Aquinas, and even Ockham. At first this had been incorporated into broad teleological cosmology and metaphysics, wherein the issue of what purposes or goals we ought to pursue made

---

Skinner's vision of human nature as lacking all free will and human dignity, it comes mighty close to doing so.

good sense. Later, however, human beings were seen by many as an utterly unique phenomenon here on earth—a hybrid of divine and mundane substance—though, of course, everybody acknowledged that we bled, had to eat, and did much that other animals did as well. Nevertheless, our having a mind appears to have been such a shocking, awesome fact that it was pretty much believed by all the intellectuals that human beings really are not ultimately of this earth. Augustine exclaimed, "How great, my God, is this force of memory, how exceedingly great! It is like a vast and boundless subterranean shrine. . . . Yet this is a faculty of my mind and belongs to my nature; nor can I myself grasp all that I am. Therefore the mind is not large enough to contain itself. But where can that uncontained part of it be?"[16]

Thus the facts and principles that are of more interest to human life as such—among them the facts and principles of ethics, morality, politics, and so forth—were for many centuries considered to be ones related to spirituality. Arguably, in the age of enormous scientific and technological success, this did not bode well for such concerns.

It had been relatively easy for Augustine, for example, qua ontologist, to make room for freedom of the will. He was not constrained in this by any loyalty to materialism, even though Augustine was beginning to reject the influential dualist thinking of Manichaeism. Indeed, even in our day, most people receive their ethical and moral teachings from church, not from science, and relate values in general to a supposed nonnatural or spiritual realm. This we've seen is largely because the naturalistic framework is infected with a reductive materialist ontology and thus cannot yield a coherent account of human causal agency, of purposiveness, and thus, ultimately, of moral responsibility.

As science gradually made its gains on this spiritualistic approach to human life, indeed to an understanding of the whole universe, not only was the idealistic otherworldly focus beginning to recede for many of the most formidable minds but morality also became de-

16. Augustine, *Confessions* (New York: Vintage Books, 1998), p. 8ff.

throned from its earlier lofty place. Ethics proper began to occupy a less prominent position in our educated, academic culture. Human beings were beginning to be viewed as really just more complicated physical beings. Everything was ultimately thought of as governed by the principles of classical mechanics, that is, the physics that ultimately was given its major expression in the work of Isaac Newton. In Hobbes, we have only moral psychology, not morality proper.[17] In Locke, morality is squeezed in with great difficulty, as is free will, and with other luminaries of empiricism morality is really explained away in various causal terms—for example, in Hume and Adam Smith.

Thus the baby was thrown out with the bathwater. To appropriate the study of nature, everything that even seemed otherworldly had been abandoned. The Hobbesian notion that human beings are by instinct inclined toward self-preservation takes the laws of motion into the realm of psychology and ultimately social philosophy.[18] The claim that after a period of life in a state of nature a social contract is entered into by which society and government are formed is founded on a mechanical physics of human life.[19] It is the application of classical materialistic (meta)physics to politics: Human beings in a state of nature, outside of civil society, are taken to be clusters of complex, intelligent matter, keeping in motion, attempting to survive. Since, however, ultimately there are too many of them, they collide, and repeated conflicts ensue. Once this happens, their higher form of ma-

---

17. In moral psychology, the phenomena we welcome instead of lament in human behavior is explained by reference to features of our psychology: drives, motives, passions, inclinations, and so forth. The element of intentionality, involving free thought and action, is excluded as mysterious, not consistent with universal efficient causation. Morality proper, however, requires that human beings be capable of genuine free choice, the capacity to cause their significant actions on their own, with influences given proper due but only as influences, not as causes. For more on this, see Tibor R. Machan, *A Primer on Ethics* (Norman: University of Oklahoma Press, 1997).

18. It is no accident that Hobbes spent a better part of his life arguing against the freedom of the will.

19. See Tibor R. Machan, "Why Agreement Is Not Enough" (forthcoming).

terial intelligence—something like a complex computer (one prominent model of the mind in our own time)—prompts them to make rules
that will establish peace. (Hobbes retained some of the language of
ethics or morality, of course, but by virtue of his more basic mechanistic framework, he robbed it of all conceptual support![20])

In other words, we are normally inclined, like billiard balls, to go
on moving, living, but then when we start colliding and our feedback
system tells us, "Now, sit down and make some rules," we respond
with the solution of the social contract. Once the rules are established,
just as with traffic laws, they govern our continued movement or pursuit of our self-preservation. So, essentially, the grandfather of much
of liberal political economy, Thomas Hobbes—and I say grandfather
only because he was not quite liberal: he just laid the philosophical
foundations of a certain version of liberalism—was a thoroughgoing
(i.e., reductive) materialist who wanted to apply the principles of the
physical sciences to everything. In our time this line of thinking was
perhaps most forcefully and influentially advanced by B. F. Skinner.[21]

One result was the removal of nearly all elements of morality from
the intellectual framework of a major branch of classical liberalism.
(What remained was a somewhat minor "imperative" inclining us toward self-preservation, which in economics is transformed into the
profit motive or utility maximization, with some room, for example in
Adam Smith's work, for an innate gregarious sentiment. But although
this is something like a norm,[22] it is not optional for us and thus has
no moral significance.)

20. For more on this, see Tibor R. Machan, *Classical Individualism* (London:
Routledge, 1998).
21. B. F. Skinner, *Beyond Freedom and Dignity* (New York: Bantam Books, 1973).
22. A norm is a standard by which we judge the goodness of something, say, an
apple, a seal, or a chimp. In the case of human life, some norms are, for example,
medical; others, ethical or political. Those of the latter type pertain to how we ought
to act, whereas those of the former, to the involuntary, nonvolitional advantages or
disadvantages we enjoy.

SCIENTISM AND CLASSICAL LIBERALISM

In this scientistic perspective, its familiar ideals—the language of blaming people for violating our rights, for example, of holding them responsible for rape or assault or kidnapping or all the less serious crimes—had been largely removed from the essential constituents of the framework of liberalism.[23] All we are, by the most fundamental tenets of this vision, is atoms moving forward, and when we collide we automatically adjust and proceed more smoothly and peacefully. That is how society and its laws were supposed to have come about; at least, this seemed like a useful hypothesis for understanding human life and society. Any mishap in the process is entirely attributable to our lack of sufficient information, not to evil, irresponsible, negligent, or vicious conduct. No personal moral responsibility could be involved in how things turn out in society (just as so many claim today, from academic psychologists to guests on tabloid television talk shows).

Of course, this view did not affect everything, since not everybody held it, and even those who did were of somewhat varying minds about it. Clearly the position did not completely eliminate blaming or praising—for one thing, if you did not hold these beliefs, you would be blamed for being foolish or stubborn! Still, the scientistic outlook became very prominent. According to some, capitalism itself ultimately rested on it.

Adam Smith, when he wrote *The Wealth of Nations*, essentially took the Hobbesian idea a step further and said not only that at least

23. It is not that the language of ethics had been fully purged—clearly in the personal lives of the thinkers, then or now, such language cannot but make its appearance. The trouble is that the foundations of classical liberalism had been very inhospitable to that language. It is interesting to see how Skinner tried to expunge that language once and for all. Classical liberals in our time avoid this but try the alternative tactic of reconceiving the meaning of ethical and moral language along lines of emotivism—via defining "we ought" or "we should" as "we prefer" or "we approve."

in commerce we are all embarking on promoting our self-interest but also that the less government there is, the better this system is going to work for our prosperity. This is because government intervention and regulation amount to the introduction of friction into human social life, unless all it does is keep the peace. Accordingly, the whole notion of the free-market economic system owes a great deal to this tradition of scientism, of lifting the principles of the physical sciences and applying them to human behavior. Subjectivism in ethics, another tenet of a good portion of classical liberalism—the idea that all judgments of right and wrong are expressions of private feelings, preferences, or desires—is really driven by this scientistic outlook. Scientism does not allow for objective moral values because the notion of right and wrong conduct does not make sense if no options exist and all we can do is what we have to. Even plain value judgments—as to whether something is good or bad, for example, a good apple or a bad stomach—are deemed to be a matter of personal preference or aversion. Here is how Hobbes put the point originally: "But whatsoever is the object of any man's appetite or desire, that is it which he for his part calleth good: and the object of his hate and aversion, evil. . . . For these words of good and evil . . . are ever used with relation to the person that useth them: there being nothing simply and absolutely so; nor any common rule of good and evil. . . ."[24]

This view was for a long time shared by the greatest of classical liberal economists, the main friends of the free market in academe, via their embrace of the "subjective theory of value." For example, Don Bellante points out that given that "the values and motives of individuals [are] entirely subjective it is impossible for an analyst to pass judgment on the optimality of the individual's chosen actions."[25]

---

24. Thomas Hobbes, *Leviathan* (Baltimore, Md.: Penguin Books, 1968), p. 120.

25. Don Ballante, "Subjective Value Theory and Government Intervention in the Labor Market," *Austrian Economics Newsletter* (spring/summer 1989): 1–2. I discuss how the free-market economist could continue to uphold the principle of voluntary

In other words, actions cannot be judged right or wrong except by subjective standards—those the individual embraces for himself or herself. The idea is expressed in aesthetics as "beauty is in the eye of the beholder."

Accordingly, right and wrong conduct, too, had been thought a matter of how a person takes it, no more, at least so far as the economist is concerned with human behavior. Within pure economic analysis this stance could be quite appropriate. Since, however, economists have always been called upon to offer general commentary on political-economic matters, not just strict economic analyses, they have often taken this value-free framework with them into their studies of and recommendations pertaining to public policy matters—environmental, racial, and other topics. In these areas their value-free approach had always sat badly with most people simply because human life is necessarily normative and value-laden.[26] But what was widely resisted among the broader public did not begin to become respectable until the late twentieth century. Logically, of course, such doubts should have been evident from the outset of scientism's popularity, since the debate between positive and normative analysts itself rests on the underlying view that there is one right and many wrong ways to go about thinking about human affairs. Holding one's adversaries guilty of bad thinking is an inescapably normative point.

---

exchange even if it were possible "for an analyst to pass judgment on the optimality of the individual's chosen actions," as this is deemed possible by cognitivist moral theorists. See Tibor R. Machan, *Capitalism and Individualism: Reframing the Argument for the Free Society* (New York: St. Martin's Press, 1990). See also Tibor R. Machan, "Individual versus Subjective Values," *International Journal of Social Economics* 16 (1989): 49–59, and "Why it Appears That Objective Moral Claims Are Subjective," *Philosophia* 26 (nos. 1–4, 1997): 1–23.

26. To discern why this is so, one need but consider that in any argument, including one about this very topic, it is implicit that one side believes the other has gone wrong, ought to have gone another way; and that is a normative point.

SCIENTISM AND MORALITY,
A MARRIAGE ON THE ROCKS

In the early twentieth century even the few free-market economists who overtly attacked some versions of scientism reintroduced it by the back door, for example, by way of modeling the market along lines of more complex physical systems. This is indeed a competing approach in our own time, what with so many efforts to model human social life on quantum mechanics, chaos theory, the behavior of termites, and so forth.

Despite what F. A. Hayek argued—that in fact the modeling went the other way, so that, for example, Charles Darwin adopted the framework of social scientists such as Adam Ferguson by which to understand natural phenomena—the basic grounding remained scientism. The social theory of Bernard Mandeville and David Hume had, by that time, been placed under the influence of a more complex version of scientism. It is one that retained the foremost ingredient of the earlier, mechanistic type—determinism, the denying of the possibility of free choice, self-governance, or bona fide initiative in human life. For example, Ferguson held that we are motivated by "subrational drives." In turn, Hayek claimed that Ferguson, "with his phrase about 'the results of human action but not of human design' has provided . . . the best definition of the task of all social theory."[27]

The crucial point about scientism is its thoroughgoing determinism, its denial that human beings are agents, its relegation of human reasoning into the service of the human passions, so that cognition and self-regulation in light of understanding play no role in the explanation of human action. What matters is the simple or complex ways we are driven to behave.

In contrast, bona fide science and norms are perfectly compatible

---

27. F. A. Hayek, "Dr. Bernard Mandavelle," in C. Nishiyama and K. L. Leube, eds., *The Essence of Hayek* (Stanford, Calif.: Hoover Institution Press, 1984), p. 189.

because the former must accept whatever there is to be found in reality, including beings whose nature includes a normative component or dimension, even a moral one. Thus Aristotle could call ethics a science because he was not being reductive in his approach to the sciences, as scientism has always been.

THE MORAL VIEWPOINT VERSUS SCIENTISM

At first scientism seemed to offer support for freedom, because its idea was that with less intervention in their lives by other persons, including governments, people would move about efficiently. Laissez-faire public policy is in a way like frictionless space, posing the least resistance to human motion and progress. Without government regulation, coercion, and interference, human beings would advance more rapidly toward self-preservation and self-enhancement. It makes rather good sense.

In our day, however, a fairly vocal group of academic philosophers, taking their cues from a wide array of past moral and political thinkers, have begun to revitalize the moral case for classical liberalism, one that had been largely silenced by scientism's earlier triumph. Mainly they have found that the older view left us with serious dilemmas, especially when we set about to attempt to defend the institutions it hoped to recommend. In short, the moral dimension of human social life began to be seen as irrepressible.

This newly emerging moral viewpoint that has energized many classical liberals treats human beings as agents of their own conduct, as crucial first causes of some of what they do. Such an idea had major problems associated with it in the past, when efficient causation was thought the only kind worthy of the name. Since with human beings the talk about what they ought to do has persisted, resisting all efforts to reconstruct moral language into some kind of technology, and since science has itself undergone some major changes, the prospects for a moral defense of the free society are no better than they were in the past.

Moral talk does not appear to apply to other animals, although there are, of course, some who would say otherwise. It seems right that when a dog bites the mail carrier, we do not believe it ought not to have done that, even as we lament the fact. We do not treat the dog as a responsible agent, as if it could have made a different choice and thus might not have bitten the carrier. We do continue to treat human beings as responsible, not as a robot or brute with no choice about what it will do, good or bad. Certainly, however, if we are indeed what the essence of scientism contends—mechanical or, these days, computational systems—and we just behave as we do with no choice about the matter, then we cannot be held responsible, for better or for worse.[28]

SCIENTISM IS NOT ENOUGH FOR
POLITICAL ECONOMY

The problem is that in the human realm, the classical liberal must always consider something like the following: "Since, as liberalism sees it, governments obstruct progress, we should or ought to, or it is right for us to, reduce government intervention, so government intervention is wrong." They go on to propose in their writings that coercion, government regimentation, is unjust, be it in regard to matters of fighting crime, handling the suppression of dissident literature, or planning people's economic activities. Although it seems inescapable for us to think and say such things—for even to recommend the mech-

---

28. If scientism as derived from the natural sciences were true, human beings, too, would be bundles of inert particles being moved about in the universe, and there would be no question of right or wrong about what they do, nor about what they believe (which is one area in which scientism leads to serious difficulties, since it is unable to make sense of people being wrong, even as to what they think).

anistic framework involves saying, "This is how we ought to think"—
that kind of thinking and talk makes no sense within the scientistic
framework.

Here is where the central flaw in the scientistic approach to politics comes into clear focus, and it was one of classical liberalism's
champions, George Stigler, who brought attention to it: If everything
is governed by deterministic laws, then there is no right and wrong
about anything, including, of course, tyranny and government regulation, intervention, crimes, and so forth.[29]

So, ironically, the champions of classical liberalism, influenced
by this scientistic outlook, had deprived themselves philosophically of
the very ideas, namely, moral analysis and in its wake exhortation,
that could possibly undermine government tyranny and intervention.
This is because the only way you can battle something that people do
wrong is to see it as something that might have been done differently
and could be changed by them, if they are convinced by arguments
showing it to be true, in the future. If moral truth does not exist and its
purported language is merely a guide for the expression of sentiments,
preferences, biases, and tastes, then such convictions can never be
achieved. Preferences may change, but by this account not because
one is convinced that they are wrong and that one ought to prefer
something else.

One element of classical liberalism, as an example, is that slavery

29. Stigler, a Nobel laureate in economics and a supporter of deregulation, bit the
bullet and accepted the consequences of this Hobbesian, scientific approach to human
life. He was a great champion of the free market. Yet he also accepted the consequences of scientism. In one of his talks, at the Mt. Pelerin Society, he argued that we
live in the best of all possible worlds! Why? Well, because there is no other possibility.
Since there is no choice about what we will do, the world we live in is the world that
came about through the laws of nature. There is no other way that it could be. So
blaming people, including governments, is entirely futile. It is like protesting the
weather or one's height or age.

is morally corrupt.[30] It exists, but it might not have existed had people done things differently, and it might not continue if they choose to act differently in the future. Without the availability of the intellectual stance that renders such a position meaningful and true, all we can do is describe how things happened, are going on, and will develop, we do in astronomy or evolutionary biology. Fretting about how it might have happened and should turn out is irrational within such a perspective. Suppose it is impossible for people to do anything differently—they must do the things they do, if this is a deterministic universe through and through such that we lack all initiative. Then all we can do is look at slavery and say that is how it has to be, as when our picnic is rained out. We can lament it, but we cannot meaningfully say that no one ought to be a master! Nor can we rationally say to politicians, presidents, criminals, or terrorists that they should not act the way they are acting or do what they are doing. We simply have to accept their behavior, describe it, and make predictions based on what we have learned. Such is the influence scientism has had on how we view human affairs.

In contemporary classical liberal or libertarian thought, all this has been understood to have a destructive impact on the prospect of human liberty. That individuals have the right to liberty—to trade their wares, acquire property, enter into and freely consent to a contract, resist thievery and tyranny (including being intruded upon by governmental prior restraint)—makes no sense if someone who violates those rights is doing just what he or she must do. It may be bad, but it cannot be wrong! Yet violation of rights is just that and assumes the violator can do otherwise.

The indictments against such conduct become, then, expressions

---

30. Perhaps the best example of the expression of this in earlier times, from a classical liberal perspective, can be found in John Trenchard and Thomas Gordon, *Cato's Letters; or, Essays on Liberty, Civil and Religious, and Other Important Subjects*, 2 vols. (Indianapolis, Ind.: Liberty Fund, 1995).

of our wishes. Of course, our wishes go against the wishes of those who do want to tyrannize us, intrude on us, kill us, steal from and regulate us, but there is no valid issue of who is right and who is wrong because it all just happens, for better or for worse.

Freedom cannot be defended if it is not a matter of a genuine human option whether you respect people's right to freedom. If a tyrant, regulator, or politician cannot help, for example, intruding on people, if it is indeed an unavoidable fact that somebody murders someone, then it cannot even be called murder, merely a killing. It is no different from when a hyena attacks a zebra. A zebra cannot say or think, nor can we think this about the hyena, that it ought not to do this, it is wrong. It makes no sense. Indeed, it does not even make sense to put to others that their thinking is flawed, that they ought to have reached different conclusions from those they did reach, since everyone does exactly what he or she must do. Criticism, even in a philosophical or scholarly context, is nonsense: No one could do better or worse than he or she in fact does.

Most classical liberals today recognize that if human beings were automatons, instinctually driven, material, pulsating things, then it cannot be true ever to say that what they are doing is wrong. Nor can we say that they ought to change their ways and pay compensation when they have done wrong—or even merely that they ought to apologize. That language, the language of norms, ethics, public policy, and any kind of action guidance, is completely ruled out. It is no different from demonology, witchcraft, astrology, or alchemy. Just as all these are bogus disciplines, so must political philosophy, political economy, ethics, and public policy become bogus fields, if the scientistic approach is true.

But—and this is the crucial question to raise—is the scientistic approach sound? is scientism true? Are the contemporary classical liberals or libertarians right? Can their ideals be supported based on a sound philosophy in which the normative dimensions of human life are included, given firm footing? We have already noted some problems, so let us see why there are further serious doubts about it.

ADDITIONAL FLAWS OF SCIENTISM

A further major problem understood by now with the scientistic approach is that it actually violates the most important tenets of science, that we should consider the evidence as it is and not impose a framework from some other area in which the evidence may not apply to the subject matter we are interested in understanding. If we are studying the psychology of rats and then we apply the findings to teenagers, we are likely to go wrong.

Not that there could not be some help there. Sometimes there are aspects of rat psychology that we share, but there are also aspects we do not share, just as we fall exactly the way a sack of potatoes falls from the top of a building. There is little difference between the fall of a person and that of a sack of potatoes, but it does not mean that a person *is* a sack of potatoes, only that the *truths* that apply to the sack of potatoes also apply to the person. Some of the findings of some of the sciences can be applied to some other subjects, but it is a very delicate process, and it has been driven, throughout the past four hundred years of Western civilization, by a lot more hope than evidence.

Just as the natural sciences improved our ability to manipulate nature—to control it and to extract from it all sorts of benefits for ourselves—the hope was that we could do the same in ethics, politics, and so on. The assumption was made: If we only knew the laws that drive human beings to do what they do, we could apply social engineering to human life and improve it. But that hope was not fulfilled, as we now well know.

There are other obvious difficulties with scientism and its application to social policy. Nearly a century of scientism and 150 years of social science have not really improved the world morally, not at least outside of the realm of technology itself, where it had its home in the first place. The Nazis, the Soviets, the hoods, the child molesters, rapists, serial killers, and the like were not rehabilitated or repelled by means of social engineering. At most, things got no worse than they have always been, except, again, where technology applies directly, as in handling household chores or producing the information highway or curing the sick.

We also know that 150 years of interventionist economics, which is also based on Keynesian, Marxian, Galbraithian, and other social science, did not improve the world much; quite the contrary. It has left us as confused as we were to start with, at least as a general rule, throughout the globe.

RETURNING TO PROPER SCIENCE

What many contemporary classical liberal thinkers, or a handful of them at least, have come to see is that what is necessary to make amends for the oversights of scientism is to become properly scientific.

As we have noted, following Aristotle, this would first require understanding science as a process of discovery. It is not the laying down of prerequisites of what things must be, which is the province of metaphysics and ontology, both of which are usually minimalist in their scope precisely for this reason: The prerequisites of existence or being are very few.

It would, furthermore, amount to the recognition, first of all, that this animal species we call the human being has certain unique attributes, ones that cannot be derived from our understanding of other features of reality. We would learn that just because there are some things we share with the rat, the computer, or the North Star, it does not follow that we are just like those entities, that we share their basic nature or essence. A proper scientific approach reveals that with the emergence of the human species some unique attributes have emerged in nature.

HUMAN NATURE—SANS SCIENTISM, VIA SCIENCE

The foremost of these unique attributes is that human beings can think, and this is an activity that cannot be automatic. At first, this is something we know from plain common sense. To any parent or teacher this should be obvious. Those who have dealt with children or students cannot deny that one cannot force them to think. That contribution to the rearing or educational process has to be provided by the child or student. They have to will it to happen. If they do not, it is not going to happen. You can wear funny hats, you can sing songs, you can do all sorts of tricks, but they are not going to pay attention until they choose to do so on their own initiative—because it is up to them to do it.

More technical reflection also affirms that this is a unique aspect of human beings. They produce ideas, theories, and novelty throughout the parameters of their lives, and none of that can be adequately explained by reference to mere external stimuli or genetic constitution. Human beings initiate some of what they do. Much of what is crucial to their lives is not simply the result of previous forces working on them.

As earlier noted, Roger W. Sperry devoted his postlaureate life to demonstrating, by the tools of his particular science, that there is actually a physiological basis for freedom of the will—indeed, that free will is the power of the cerebral cortex to govern the function of the rest of the human brain.

Sperry argued, as we've seen, that human beings have the kind of brain in which a higher portion monitors and controls much of human behavior even when some portions of the lower brain might incline one in a given direction. This is consistent with common sense: We have inclinations, desires, wishes, and habits. But we can watch over these and we can guide ourselves away from or in line with them. We may want to eat more than we finally decide we should. So we stop.

That does not mean that our inclination is not there. It means that our higher brain functions are capable of monitoring and altering our inclinations. This is what we call self-restraint. This is resisting temptation.

MORAL RESPONSIBILITY

Many of the people in academe, as well as those who end up on *Oprah*, *Geraldo*, or *Charlie Rose*, have tended to overlook a simple but powerful point about people. Most of those who do wrong are voluntarily yielding to the temptation to evade facts, to let themselves be motivated by various strong emotions, and to fail to resist flawed ideas as to how they ought to proceed in life. Instead, they are often treated by students of human affairs as if they were just like the special, rare cases in which individuals have to carry on as they do for reasons over which they have no control. (The fact that they are put in jail may be an additional wrinkle in this story that has not been told yet. But I'm sure that we will eventually have judges appearing on TV who say, well, we can't help ourselves, we just have to put these social misfits in jail. They may say, "We are addicted to jailing people.")

Criticism of any position implies not only, as noted before, that one might have done otherwise but also that some criteria are being applied to which adherence is required. And if we deny the capacity for human initiative, there is no way to make sense of criticism, in the last analysis: One's insistence on following certain standards would also be the result of nothing more than certain forces that make one insist on it. Those who would deny those standards would have as valid a ground for that as those who embrace them. All propositions, in the end, would turn out to be equally sound, equally true, which would produce intellectual chaos.

MORAL CHAOS VERSUS THE NORMATIVE
CASE FOR LIBERTY

In a sense this result has actually been achieved in certain circles. Multiculturalism is distinguished, in part, for insisting on the impossibility of making any distinction between cultures that are better and those that are worse, even in their understanding of the world. That this is itself a claim to a better understanding of the world does not seem to disturb the proponents of the position. We can learn from it at least that the implications of the deterministic, value-free approach are quite drastic and intellectually intolerable. Truth itself dies once freedom is denied.

So we can affirm human initiative without violating science or the tenets of coherence. What are the broad political implications of this?

We start with noticing that unless they were terribly abused, human beings have the capacity to make free choices. They actually can initiate some of their conduct, and their conduct, moreover, is not fully explainable by reference to past events. From this it follows that human beings have to learn to act because they are not given prompters, instincts, which tell them what to do. Put generally, we all, except for the crucially incapacitated, have to learn to live right.

This accords with most of the cultural practices throughout human societies and history. We send people to school. We do not expect them to acquire knowledge of chemistry or computer science or philosophy by instinct in the way that most birds and bees acquire most of their behavior through instincts.

Furthermore, another implication of this understanding of human nature is that we are self-responsible creatures, and that we must individually produce a great deal of what is important in our lives. We have to play a very decisive role in what happens in our lives. If we do not, we do not learn. We do not realize the cost of mistakes. They come back to haunt us. We can notice this in the course of discussing the topic at hand. If someone disagrees, the implication is that one has argued badly. If someone agrees, the implication is that one has argued correctly. One is held responsible for either.

FROM INDIVIDUAL RESPONSIBILITY TO THE FREE SOCIETY

When we consider what self-responsibility implies, the notion of liberty starts creeping into our vocabulary. It turns out that this self-responsibility requires, in a social community context, that people have their own private jurisdiction in which both their achievements and their failures are within their own domain and not dumped on others. Here one can notice the implications for environmental ethics and politics. Human beings, who are self-responsible, who can create as well as destroy, need to have their own dominion, their own private property wherein their achievements and mistakes take effect. That implies, for a legal system, that the institution of private property is essentially a humanistic institution. Everyone must have a private domain, a sovereign status, within society, one that others must respect and that governments are established to protect. It is appropriate to our nature as human beings not primarily, as economists argue, because it leads to prosperity, not because it leads to creativity, but mainly because it accords with our human nature as self-responsible, moral agents.

We human beings need to know what props are available with which to guide our lives and make choices. We human beings need to know whether, when we want to be charitable, we can take Jim's telephone and give it to somebody, or if it is only our own tape recorder that we can give to somebody. If we all get confused about this, as we do in societies without private property, then the requirements of our humanity are not being met. Such a society is literally demoralized.

Throughout Western intellectual history, it has been mostly religion that has stressed the moral nature of human life. Of course, Christianity learned this from the Greeks and Romans, who had something of this in mind already. Socrates emphasized the virtuous human life, as did Aristotle. Both saw that some measure of individual responsibility and liberty are necessary conditions of society. Both the secular natural-law tradition and the Christian stress on each person's responsibility to save his or her soul imply the free society. From the secular viewpoint, however, these implications were suppressed by scientism. And within the religious framework the frequent zeal to make everyone conform to God's will tended to extinguish the libertarian implications.

In the last analysis, the free society has two strong traditions advancing its defense. The scientistic approach reigned supreme in earlier times. In ours it is the normative approach that is gaining prominence. To decisively determine which of these is the better, which is true, is a topic for a much longer and more detailed discussion.[31] But we can already see that there is no obvious superiority to the scientistically inspired position that denies freedom of the will, ethics, and normative politics in human life. It seems, also, that the normative view stands a better chance of being a successful intellectual defense of the free society.

What can be said in reply to MacIntyre, accepting his comment on its face as a sincere lamentation about something possibly devious in the liberal tradition? For one, the attempts, following Hobbes, to reduce all understanding of human affairs to physics, in the last analysis—which today emerges as the extreme mathematization of economics and some other social sciences—could be taken as a ploy, a way to avoid the hard questions. Put plainly, by construing all human action as driven by the profit motive or utility maximization, the question of whether it is right or good to vigorously pursue profit is avoided. If wealth maximization is an innate drive, if survival is an innate drive,

31. Machan, *Capitalism and Individualism*. See also Tibor R. Machan, "Reason in Economics versus Ethics," *International Journal of Social Economics* 22 (No. 7, 1995): 19–37.

then no one needs to prove that it is a good thing, and the argument is won before it begins. Then, also, a subjective value theory enables us to avoid many tough issues in ethics and politics, and the view that such a theory leads to liberalism becomes, once again, a kind of ploy.

The fact that this ploy is played out by Marx just as vigorously as it was by Smith and his neoclassical or Austrian economic followers may indicate, however, that what we have witnessed is not so much self-deception as the desperate effort to remain true to a misguided paradigm of intellectual respectability: scientism. Furthermore, all along we could also witness a defense of liberalism that avoided these mistakes, the natural-law classical liberal tradition. It is this tradition that has become reinforced in very promising ways by the work of twentieth-century classical liberal political theorists.

Thus it would appear that MacIntyre's ire is highly selective: On all fronts essentially normative theses had been advanced in scientistic garb, whether socialist or liberal. It is my contention here that once the contemporary normative case for liberalism is fully appreciated, it can be seen as a most successful attempt to understand human community life, not in the slightest inconsistent either with proper science or with reasonable moral sensibilities.

CHAPTER FIVE

Hayek's Unintended Scientism

ROADS TO TRUTH

There are different approaches to reaching similar conclusions, although not all are equally sound. The foregoing case for the free society takes a normative approach. In other words, it is argued that a polity in which the right to individual liberty is upheld is better for human beings living in communities than in competing systems. It follows, also, that this view ought to be embraced and implemented wherever and whenever it is possible for people to do so. This view rests, furthermore, on a more basic fact about human beings. This is that they are capable of initiative and have the responsibility to choose well in their lives.

Far more prominent and respectable are defenses of the free society that eschew the normative dimension. F. A. Hayek developed such a nonnormative case, as did others such as Milton Friedman, Ludwig von Mises, and George Stigler. Although these theorists differ among themselves a great deal, they are united by the belief that resting political arguments on normative theories is not as productive as approaching the topic in a purely positive, descriptive way.

I wish to examine Hayek's case and then contrast it with the one implicit in the preceding discussion. I propose to show that Hayek's case is not sound and that one that takes the normative dimensions of human life seriously is superior. A major reason Hayek's approach is flawed is its refusal to face the fact of human initiative. And once initiative is rejected or omitted, the normative approach must also be avoided. Yet such an approach to politics, I think, faces serious problems.

HAYEK'S CASE FOR THE FREE SYSTEM

Does reason recommend freedom? Is the idea of a rational moral standard compatible with the free political order? There are both critics and advocates of the free society who answer these questions in the negative. Among those dismayed with the kind of support traditionally given to liberal political theory and institutions we find theorists from both the Right and the Left. Not only Marxists and other socialists but also conservatives such as Thomas Molnar, Walter Berns, Marc F. Plattner, and Irving Kristol object to liberalism. They are concerned primarily with the spiritual and communitarian values in society and believe classical liberals give these short shrift.

Frequent disavowal of moral values by classical liberals and utilitarian economists who defend the free society gives substance to the concern of these thinkers. Indeed, freedom is often caricatured as chaos by those who would have some people "representing the state" establish order in a community. But more important is the argument of those who concede the point and then reject reason in favor of custom, habit, instinct, spontaneity, and liberty.

F. A. Hayek is among the latter. I first outline Hayek's position, then evaluate its worth as theory. I show that in terms of standards applicable either to any field of science or to the social sciences specifically, Hayek's thesis is defective.

Concerning the issue of when a theory is successful, I assume that if such a theory consistently accounts for the facts observed within the

domain of inquiry at hand—including the common-sense facts of ordinary human experience, which philosophy aims to integrate into a
comprehensive, coherent system—it is successful. When theories
stand in competition with each other, this standard will be applicable
for purposes of deciding how to rank them.[1]

Because I too have concluded that freedom is better than slavery,
that the free society, with its emphasis on political and economic
liberty, is superior to others, my discussion includes an outline of a
defense of conclusions I share with Hayek. I am all the more ready to
supply this alternative, given the eagerness with which some enemies
of the free society have focused on Hayek's value-free case for liberty.
Although several individuals throughout history have argued for liberty on moral grounds, the statists usually manage to ignore their case
and focus instead on such defenses of liberty as Hayek's, dismissing
it in the end for its lack of concern with virtue, justice, and morality
in general.

From the ensuing discussion, critics of the free society may see
just how compatible freedom is not only with reason but also with
virtue, justice, and morality.

SPONTANEOUS ORDER AND HUMAN REASON

The best sketch of Hayek's position is provided by the author
himself:

> The preservation of a society of free man depends on three funda-
> mental insights which have never been adequately expounded. . . .
> The first of these is that a self-generating or spontaneous order and
> organization are distinct, and that their distinctiveness is related to
> the two different kinds of rules or laws which prevail in them. The
> second is that what today is generally regarded as "social" or dis-

---

1. See Machan, *The Pseudo-Science of B. F. Skinner* (New Rochelle, N.Y.: Arlington House Publishing Co., 1974).

tributive justice has meaning only within the second of these kinds of order, the organization; but that it is meaningless in, and wholly incompatible with, that spontaneous order which Adam Smith called "the Great Society," and Sir Karl Popper called "the Open Society." The third is that the predominant model of liberal democratic institutions, in which the same representative body lays down the rules of just conduct and directs government, necessarily leads to a gradual transformation of the spontaneous order of a free society into a totalitarian system conducted in the service of some coalition of organized interest.[2]

To begin an appreciation of Hayek's ideas, it is evident that we must understand some of the central concepts in his analysis. Of these, the concept of a spontaneous order is probably most crucial.

Hayek's conception of the spontaneous order seems at first simple enough to understand.[3] In certain circumstances individual entities of a given kind behave with no deliberate plan to give their behavior a definite purpose; nevertheless, the result is an orderly pattern. A number of illustrations of such circumstances are provided by Hayek. He notes:

> There are in the physical world many instances of complex orders which we could bring about only by availing ourselves of the known forces which tend to lead to their formation, and never by deliberately placing each element in the appropriate position. . . . [Thus] iron

2. F. A. Hayek, *Law, Legislation and Liberty* (Chicago: University of Chicago Press, 1973), 1: 2.

3. Hayek makes innumerable references to what he calls the spontaneous order and its opposite, deliberate organization. See especially *Studies in Philosophy, Politics and Economics* (New York: Simon and Schuster, 1967) and *The Confusion of Language in Political Thought* (London: Institute of Economic Affairs, 1968). Crespigny summarizes Hayek's idea of the former: "This type of order does not have a purpose since it has not been deliberately created, and to agree on its desirability it is unnecessary for us to agree on the concrete results it will produce" ("F. A. Hayek: Freedom for Progress," in A. de Crespigny and K. Minogue, eds., *Contemporary Political Philosophers* [New York: Dodd, Mead, 1975], p. 53).

filings on a sheet of paper are made to arrange themselves along some of the lines of force of a magnet placed below. . . . [and] we can predict the general shape of the chains that will be formed by the filings hooking themselves together; but we cannot predict along which ones of the family of an infinite number of such curves that define the magnetic field these chains will place themselves.[4]

A spontaneous order has no designer but comes about through the operation of general rules or laws. These govern the behavior of the individual elements but do not determine the specific spatiotemporal or otherwise relevant patterns of behavior of such individual elements.

For Hayek the same is true of social life: "It would be no exaggeration to say that social theory begins with—and has an object only because of—the discovery that there exist orderly structures which are the product of the action of many men but are not the result of human design."[5] Hayek's example from social life is, as we might expect, the commercial market. He points to Adam Smith's "invisible hand," a description "in the language of his time . . . [of] how man is led 'to promote an end which was not part of his intentions.'"[6] A crucial source of support for Hayek's updated version of the invisible-hand conception of the natural or proper mode of social existence is Darwinian evolutionary theory. Although Hayek makes it clear that he rejects the cruder versions of social Darwinism, he explains that "the basic conception of evolution is still the same in both fields [biology and social theory]."[7]

Often what we have to go on in understanding Hayek's characterization of human affairs is his assertion that his own ideas have been more or less well outlined by such thinkers as Bernard Mandeville and David Hume. He also acknowledges his debt to the epistemology

4. *Studies in Philosophy*, pp. 39–40.
5. Ibid., p. 37.
6. Ibid.
7. Ibid., p. 23.

of Immanuel Kant. His reliance on the former makes it crucial for
Hayek to uphold a view of human behavior that accords with a variant
of the evolutionist theory, so that he is anxious to defend the idea that
"many of the institutions of society which are indispensable conditions
for the successful pursuit of our conscious aims are in fact the result
of customs, habits or practices which neither have been invented nor
are observed with any such purpose in view."[8] In short, such institutions and practices evolve.

In the epistemological realm, Hayek's conception of how we are
aware of reality manifests his basically Kantian framework (something
he shares with his teacher Ludwig Von Mises). Even at the basic level
of perceptual awareness Hayek concludes that human beings possess
"the capacity to act according to rules which we may be able to discover but which we need not be able to state in order to obey them."[9]
Indeed, Hayek seems to construe the action of organizing sensory and
perceptual data into a coherent structure (Gestalt) as quite automatic.[10]

The general idea is that our human way of viewing the world
provides us with virtually instinctive guidelines that "are better seen
as determining what an individual will not do rather than what he will
do."[11] These rules are comparable to the Kantian categories and intuitions of the understanding, which are structurally innate for any human mind and are supposed to operate whether we are conscious of
them or not. Hayek himself indicates his Kantian view when he tells
us, "Abstraction is not something which the mind produces by processes of logic from its perception of reality, but is rather a property of

8. Ibid., p. 11. Recall here our discussion in chapter 1 of whether evolution can
make room for free will and human initiative.

9. F. A. Hayek, *Studies in Philosophy, Politics and Economics*, p. 44.

10. Ibid., p. 45; F. A. Hayek, *The Sensory Order* (Chicago: University of Chicago
Press, 1952), pp. 52–54.

11. Hayek, *Studies in Philosophy, Politics and Economics*, p. 57.

the categories with which it operates—not a product of the mind but rather what constitutes the mind."[12]

To appreciate the significance of Hayek's epistemological position, one would have to consider in detail the point of view with which it is contrasted, the background against which he develops his own position. Hayek wants to discredit what he identifies as a Cartesian view of rationalism, namely constructivism. Within the latter, "Reason was defined as logical deduction from explicit premises, rational action . . . came to mean only such action as was determined entirely by known and demonstrable truths. . . . Institutions and practices which have not been designed in this manner can be beneficial only by accident."[13]

According to this view, "Man's reason alone should enable him to construct society anew,"[14] but Hayek presents a position in which habit, custom, and practice have a far more prominent place than that of successful action based on logical deduction from explicit premises. Although Hayek notes the existence of a conception of reason different from the Cartesian one, he presents his analysis in terms of the above alternatives.[15]

PROBLEMS IN HAYEK'S POSITION

In my criticism of Hayek I first focus on the grounds he invokes for his own approach to social theory. He tell us, "If what is called *Sprachgefuhl* (the feeling for language, for correct versus incorrect language use) consists in our capacity to follow yet unformulated rules, there is no reason why, for example, the sense of justice (the *Rechts-*

12. Hayek, *The Confusion of Language*, p. 30.
13. Ibid., p. 10.
14. Ibid.
15. Hayek, *Studies in Philosophy*, p. 94; *The Confusion of Language*, p. 21.

gefuhl) should not also consist in such a capacity to follow rules which we do not know in the sense that we can state them."[16]

Yet consider also his point that the "scientistic" attitude "is decidedly unscientific in the true sense of the word, since it involves a mechanical and uncritical application of habits of thought to fields different from those in which they have been formed."[17]

If Hayek is right in his indictment of positivist scientism (though one can hardly call all positivists uncritical), he nevertheless falls prey to a fault similar to theirs. He clearly conflates the biological and social realms by his "application of habits of thought to" these two fields when he makes use of Darwinian evolutionary theory for the purpose of understanding the phenomena studied in each. Hayek protests that Darwinian ideas had their origin in social theorizing. But that is irrelevant; he invokes the Darwinian approach as support for his conclusions about social affairs.

Even when Hayek invokes the ideas of students of human affairs such as Sapir, R. B. Lees, and Polanyi,[18] he does not escape some decisive philosophical difficulties. The second main problem Hayek faces may be referred to as self-referential inconsistency. As already noted, the standard in terms of which we can detect whether a theorist faces this problem is clearly stated by D. Bannister: A theorist "cannot present a picture of man which patently contradicts his behavior in presenting that picture."[19]

Is Hayek self-referentially inconsistent? His conception of human actions suggests such a problem. At the fundamental level Hayek appears to view human action as governed by general laws and rules that people do not invoke by choice. These laws and rules are just

16. Hayek, *Studies in Philosophy*, p. 45.

17. F. A. Hayek, *The Counter-Revolution of Science* (Glencoe, Ill.: Free Press, 1955), p. 15

18. Ibid., pp. 43–65.

19. D. Bannister, in Robert Borger and Frank Cioffi, eds., *Explanation in the Behavioral Sciences* (New York: Cambridge University Press, 1970), p. 417.

adopted or, later, just followed. As Hayek puts the point: "Learning from experience, among men no less than among animals, is a process not primarily of reasoning but of the observance, spreading, transmission and development of practices which have prevailed because they were successful—often not because they conferred any recognizable benefit on the acting individual but because they increased the chances of survival of the group to which he belonged."[20] Aside from its dubious reference to what explains learning in human life, Hayek seems, at least on the surface, to deny any genuine freedom of choice for human beings. He does not explicitly treat the issue, and he does make use of the concept "choice" when he refers to deliberate planning or selection from among alternatives. Still, a close look shows that nowhere in his analysis is there room for free will, man's capacity to initiate action. On the contrary, for Hayek, human behavior is mostly outside human control.

The crucial issue then is how Hayek conceives of human action in its most essential respects. The bulk of human affairs is viewed by him as governed by laws and rules that are not and cannot be of our choosing. People rarely if ever turn out to be agents of their actions in Hayek's framework. In accordance with the Darwinian model, human actions spring from a sort of evolutionary force that produces habits, customs, and practices that prevail (because they support group survival) over others as the driving factors in the lives of the members of any species of animals, including human beings. Even what Hayek calls conscious, deliberate choices must then be explained by reference to this Darwinian hypothesis; those that prevail must be those with survival value. Moreover, the sort of choice involved in this conscious deliberative process seems to be a kind of selection, not an initiation. In other words, at the point where Hayek admits the existence of human choice, the choice amounts to an act of selection. This could commit him to no more than an acknowledgment that we behave

20. Hayek, *Law, Legislation and Liberty*, p. 18.

in one way rather than in other ways when confronted by several alternatives we are aware of. This could be compared to the "action" taken by computers, not an act of initiation or human causation that proponents of free will have in mind. This latter idea means that human beings are originating some behavior that they might not have originated and that it is up to them whether they do one or the other. In short, there are first causes of their conduct.

Hayek's use of Darwinian theory may itself be questionable in view of the many recent discoveries concerning the Darwinian method as opposed to Darwin's theories. I take it, however, that Hayek has in mind something that is not very complicated, namely, that nature somehow favors that which overcomes more effectively and lastingly the obstacles it faces. This same idea may be invoked for the purpose of understanding the relationship between sound and unsound, acceptable and unacceptable ideas. But more pertinently, the idea could serve to explain why individuals retain some beliefs and do not retain others, even which sensory data they have found worth employing and which they have rejected. In any of these instances we have a deterministic account of human actions, whether on the cultural or the individual level.

What we have here, if I am right, is a denial of human capacity to initiate action, to exercise genuine choice, to enter spontaneously upon some behavior; and if so, then Hayek's own activities as a theoretician must be explained by reference to the same scheme. But the self-determinist free-will thesis seems to be indispensable for purposes of rendering intelligible the facts of human knowledge and rationality (including the distinguishability, on sound grounds, of truth and falsehood). According to this view, rational choice of selection from among competing theories is impossible if human beings are incapable of initiating action, and what Hayek proposes would thus appear to be internally inconsistent. I do not impose my own doctrine of free will on Hayek—his own theoretical activity theoretically presupposes that doctrine in that he surely regards what he proposes as true and demonstrable. Yet his own theory of human action appears to contradict this indispensable, even if only implicit, presupposition. That is because it is a product of survival mechanism, as his account implies! Therefore, it is not acceptable, given that other accounts he finds to be false are of a similar mechanical origin. No one can tell which is better or truer, given that all have survived.

The third problem we should note is that Hayek seems to draw a false dichotomy between spontaneous rule-obeying behavior and self-consciously planned conduct. Since the spontaneity that gives rise to a corresponding order is at least quasiautomatic, such behavior is not said to be guided by reasoning. Even though Hayek admits that conceptions of human rationality vary and do not at all rely on the Cartesian view, he does not leave room for reasoning in other than the domain of self-consciousness. In other words, only when someone knows that he is engaging in reasoning and is aware of his own rational processes, is he believed by Hayek to be rational. This is what he intends to emphasize in his reference to deliberate, self-aware conscious process as the rational activity of the human mind. When we are simply thinking out our problems, ordering our experiences, doing our daily chores, or generally carrying on with living, we are not, by Hayek's account, either rational or nonrational. This is because in these matters we follow rules.

It seems to me inadequate to narrow reasoning or rational thinking down to self-conscious (deliberate) reasoning alone. Consider the way the criminal and the common laws conceive of the reasonable man or how we conceive of ourselves when we distinguish between acting rationally and acting irrationally. There is no commitment in either of these instances to a view such as Hayek's. Of course, when we examine whether we have carried on rationally, then we engage in a form of reasoning Hayek conceives of as rational, deliberative thought. When we have no special reason to think that we have gone astray with our thinking and acting, we might never reflect upon whether we have carried on rationally or not. Yet it is quite meaningful to characterize thinking and acting that are not self-conscious as either rational or not. Haphazard, hasty, sloppy, careless, jumbled, or erratic thinking and action could all be varieties of irrationality even if it is not the case that careful, attentive, prudent, and orderly thought and action must be self-conscious—monitored, as it were, by us as we perform it.

In his support Hayek draws on theories of language learning[21] that have noted the great facility we have for implementing rules of grammar with no self-conscious effort at rehearsing the rules. I am no expert in this field, so I cannot assess the merits of the many studies nor pass judgment on the relative success of the many competing theories. Yet it seems that one could abandon a Darwinian explanatory scheme in these areas and plausibly accommodate the theories and fact Hayek invoked. One could turn to a competing idea: that human beings, from the time of infancy, can initiate the conceptual activity they are capable of. They can do this without knowing that that is what they are doing; that is, without being able to state the nature of the capacities they are using, they often do what is necessary for purposes of communication. Indeed, there are students of psychophysics and neurophysiology, such as Sperry and his followers, who maintain that the human cerebral constitution renders plausible the suggestion that conceptual processes of consciousness are essentially self-generated.

Finally, Hayek's conception of human action seems to leave no room for morality and normative political theory. Suppose that human action essentially follows rules that have emerged by the impersonal process of natural selection. Then the idea that some rules are to be obeyed or implemented and some are to be avoided or that some political systems are to be eschewed and others to be implemented— all these general ideas about what we should or should not do simply cannot make sense. If we cannot initiate these crucial forms of action, namely, those that are uniquely human, and if we are guided by rules and laws apart from our choice, then to call on us to act in one way as

21. Hayek, *Studies in Philosophy*, pp. 43–65.

opposed to another is futile. We have no say in these matters. "Ought implies can."

For example, the idea that we should eschew socialism in favor of a free market assumes that we have this capacity, that we can do it on our own, can choose to accept or reject customs, habits, and practices, however used to them many of us have become.

Although Hayek does not often employ normative concepts, he does freely call political liberty an ideal, a goal we should pursue. But his idea of human action does not appear to allow for such normative notions. On the one hand it is exclusive of self-determined action, and on the other hand, it is indeterministic. The indeterminism is basically epistemological, that is, based on the idea that complex phenomena cannot be fully known, rendering them incapable of prediction and effective centralized control. On the objective or ontological level, however, an underlying determinism emerges in Hayek's discussion of human perception and learning.

If "ought" does imply "can," if ethical edicts make sense only if one has a genuine domain of choice where one either will or will not abide by such edicts, then Hayek's avoidance of normative issues at the ethical level is quite understandable. I take it for one of my many unproven but plausible premises that a moral principle or standard could not be sound if it were impossible for human beings to choose it as a guide to concrete conduct. In short, it is my view here that morality and some variation of the freedom-of-the-will thesis are basically linked—if the former is a real feature of human life, the latter must also be. Since Hayek's endorsement of any ideal is restricted to the domain of political theory, and since the ideal of liberty seems for him to grow out of his Darwinian belief that spontaneous order is the proper order for the biological entities we are, Hayek may be said to insist on the nonnormative treatment of political affairs on principle, by virtue of the implications of his own analysis. But if this is right, Hayek cannot do what he must want to do in light of his vigorous advocacy of the free society, namely, recommend the free society and tell us we ought to accept and support it.

I have so far presented some of the difficulties I detect in Hayek's overall position. I now turn to some of the historical facts that shed light on why Hayek takes the approach he does and ends with the views he advances. After that I consider an alternative analysis in support of the free society.

HAYEK'S KANTIANISM

Both F. A. Hayek and his teacher Ludwig von Mises admit their debt to Kantian epistemology. Some of the previous points already testify to this debt. It is possible also that Hayek's avoidance of the idea of natural law can be traced to the Kantian antimetaphysical stance. (However, Hayek does remark that the earlier Greek, as opposed to later Cartesian, idea of natural law is close to his own idea of habit, custom, or practice. He even refers to Locke as an exponent of the earlier idea of natural law. Nevertheless, he eschews the concept in his positive theory.) Arguably his general skepticism about knowledge of particular entities owes much to the Kantian rejection of the possibility of knowing things-in-themselves.

In modern philosophy "natural" has generally been used to refer to that which has sensory properties, that can be perceived by sensory observation alone. In the bulk of philosophical discussions of naturalism—for example, when G. E. Moore and others speak of the "naturalistic" fallacy—it is accepted that a naturalist in ethics (or moral philosophy) believes that what is good or right must be something sensible and measurable, such as pleasure, economic welfare, and so forth. Thus "natural" does not have the meaning of "pertaining to its nature or essence" but "pertaining to that which is regularly observable about it." Post-Cartesian and especially post-Kantian philosophy had rejected naturalism qua essentials but retained naturalism qua material components, phenomena, and sensible properties.

I point out briefly that the rejection of metaphysics as first philosophy can be traced most fruitfully and prominently to Descartes. In Hobbes, too, we find a nominalist epistemology that renders knowledge of nature or reality impossible. It might best be expressed by saying that the road to nature and arguments that rested claims on nature concerned nature qua materials components, phenomena, and sensible properties. What is decisive is that the idea that essential attributes can be identified by us, known by human beings, was rejected (mainly because the model of what counts as identifying or knowing something, deductive certainty, was very strict). Although this turn from the natural qua essential to the natural qua sensible firmed up with Machiavelli (perhaps because in his era the essential nature of things had been considered supernatural!), its epistemology is best expressed by David Hume and the twentieth-century positivists. More telling is Descartes's turn inward, toward consciousness as the primary datum of knowledge. The first truth, "cogito, ergo sum," is a truth of reason, a self-evident truth that requires no reference to a reality independent of the human mind. With this significant influence philosophy thereafter tended to focus on epistemology as its primary concern. It gained priority as the fundamental area of philosophical inquiry, displacing metaphysics, in the main, to our day. Not What is reality? but What is knowledge? became the first question of philosophy.

Now it seems very likely that the empiricist ideas of Locke, Berkeley, and Hume, granting much diversity and originality, accommodated entirely this crucial turn made by Descartes. That many seventeenth- and eighteenth-century scientists continued to attest to a belief in an underlying substructure of reality is irrelevant. The grounds for such profession could be many. What is crucial is that the realm of reality capable of rational investigation was thought to be limited to the empirically confirmable or, in Kant, to the phenomenal. Empiricism first asks, How could we know? Its answer is different from the rationalists', but the issue of what domain has priority is shared by these two major theories of knowledge. (Even Hegel, very often thought to be a powerful but nonetheless basically obscure diversion—especially by Anglo-American philosophers—took Mind or Spirit or Reason as prior to matter or content or the real. That is why Marx has to turn Hegel upside down in order to make use of the dialectic in a materialist scheme.) It is clear that Kant accepted the Cartesian order of priorities. We must again ask first how knowledge is possible, then see what we know.[22] The result in Kant—here unavoidably given short shrift—was that reality is derived from the structure of human understanding, with the admission in the end that knowledge of nature or reality (in the traditional sense) is impossible. The noumenon is fully indeterminate and unidentifiable.

I think it would be more precise to say that Kant's critique of (pure) reason amounted to what is often called philosophical skepticism: The view was derived that we cannot know whether knowledge of reality exists! Perhaps we know things-in-themselves, but we could never find that we do (or do not). That is why Kant rejects all proofs for or against God's existence and counsels faith in the matter (i.e., in metaphysics).

In fairness, I should note that I believe Kant's conclusion also had a lot to do with the model of knowledge as formal, deductive certainty. For one to know reality as these philosophers wanted it (and then conclude that knowledge is impossible in such matters), one would have to *be* what one knows. To know the thing-in-itself (i.e., every entity as it is in itself), one would have to become the thing. Yet in a certain respect the demand is sound—metaphysical knowledge must have the degree of firmness these philosophers wanted. But here one might suggest that we do know the thing-in-itself (i.e., we know nature in itself, as it is essentially) by knowing our own being, by knowing ourselves as we are in ourselves.

22. Frederick L. Will, *Induction and Justification* (Ithaca, N.Y.: Cornell University Press, 1974).

So we come to Hayek. He has fought positivism with all his intellectual stamina for decades, yet Hayek and the positivists owe a common philosophical debt to Kant. Both reject metaphysics as impossible—or, in the case of the positivist, as nonsense (since statements in the field are empirically unverifiable and have no predictive capacity). Both have the view that scientific methodology must be identical in all areas of science. Positivists seem to have thought it enough to regard human affairs as complex manifestations of the components of all existent things, namely, sensory data. In Hayek's Kantian view, human affairs are still the complex phenomena of the simple sensory data of any form of existence, only now they must be understood in terms of the fixed categories of human understanding, something that logical positivists, at least, have abandoned as nonempirical. (For the logical positivists the categories are basically arbitrary constructs and are unsupported by either nature or the structure of mind.)

The intellectual and philosophical history involved in the outline I have presented is extremely complex, yet without some indication of it we cannot appreciate Hayek's position. Any cursory glance at Hayek's works will indicate how prominent a place such historical (evolutionary?) considerations have in his analyses. So despite the necessary brevity of my outline, I have arrived at a point where we can at least attempt the presentation of an alternative to Hayek's position. I have shown that Hayek's idea of spontaneity is derived from his conclusion that our knowledge of the factors operative in human affairs is and must be limited. The nature of human understanding, including the structurally imposed limitations on knowledge of particular things, implies the view that human actions are not purposive (in the sense of freely chosen) or determinate (as the reductionists among positivists would in principle have it). If the problems I have outlined render this view crucially defective for purposes of understanding human affairs, we need a better alternative. I think Hayek's problems begin with his basically antimetaphysical approach to social theory, especially the theory of human action. With this in mind, I now begin an outline of the position which to me seems sound.

That a certain position is defective does not imply that it has no valuable insights to offer or that there are any more satisfactory explanations available. What Hayek offers could indeed be the best among the numerous widely discussed approaches to political and economic affairs. My own criticism has thus far been internal, and it is not enough to answer the questions to which Hayek and others address themselves. So I note that I regard Hayek's approach as valuable, better than most, even better than that offered by another widely respected school of free-market, libertarian-oriented thinkers, the positivist or what has come to be called the Chicago school. It is inappropriate here to discuss my reasons for this comparative evaluation, but it may help to indicate some points that legitimately occur to people considering the thesis of this chapter.

In offering the outline of an alternative case for an essentially free social order, I will mention where and how it differs from Hayek's position. To start with, the position I offer rests in large part on the case for human initiative I advanced in the earlier portions of this book. I start with the contention that human beings have free will, that they can cause some of the significant actions in their lives, and that they are responsible for doing this well.

The view I offer in contrast to Hayek's takes metaphysics seriously and accords it a place of priority in an analytical scheme or a philosophical theory. For any claim of judgment whatever—about mind or society or knowledge—presupposes existence, and that fact pushes the metaphysical problem into the foreground. Descartes's thinking ego could not have been thinking had there been nothing to think about—the activity of thought not only requires some agent but also some object. Indeed, existence is an underlying fact in any inquiry, and the attempt to deny it can lead only to nonsense. A proof of the nature of knowledge, for instance, that does not acknowledge existence cannot succeed as a proof—it is a nonstarter. The premises for a proof could not be obtained if reality itself is in doubt.

I have already done what I set out to do in order to establish the grounds for my normative argument. From that much it is possible to advance to the case for a free society that invokes considerations of normativity. The nature of existence is not negligible in considering what kind of causation is possible for human beings to take part in. I am advocating an Aristotelian approach to this subject.[23]

For our purposes it is crucial that this position embrace a multispectival monism—a conception of reality as pluralistic in its manifestations but conforming to certain essential laws. The idea of causation entailed by this metaphysics is naturalistic and necessitarian. Here a crucial difference between this and Hayek's scheme appears.

No longer is cause to be construed either as a Humean regularity or as Kantian category of human understanding. Causes are real, part of nature, however difficult it may be for us to identify them and prove their existence in any given instance. Moreover, various kinds of causation may exist in nature, depending on what kinds of things are involved in causal relationships. Unlike the Humean and Kantian conceptions of scientific causation, in which the character of causes must be a function of the character of human knowledge, the present scheme proposes that the natures of the entities involved in causal encounters determine the identity of the causation.[24]

That such pluralism in causality is plausible may be appreciated by reflecting on the suggestion that thoughts, chairs, chemical compositions, and electrons are very different types of entities. They may thus interact with others in a variety of ways. When it is said that ideas produce consequences, is it warranted to expect the mode of produc-

---

23. Tibor Machan, *Human Rights and Human Liberties* (Chicago: Nelson Hall, 1975), and *Individuals and Their Rights* (Chicago: Open Court, 1989).

24. Milton Fisk, *Nature and Necessity* (Bloomington: Indiana University Press, 1973).

tion to be the same as when chairs produce backaches or pollutants produce eye irritation? Unless a reductionism is built into the methodology of studying these varied interactions—for example, by way of empiricism—the question of what kind of causation ensues can be left open to investigation.

We can now indicate how spontaneity emerges within the present schema. I have argued that within the metaphysical framework hinted at above it is no longer necessarily unscientific to hypothesize the existence of genuine free will. Instead of the doctrine of spontaneity developed with the assistance of Darwinian evolutionary theory and other ideas about the complexity of human affairs, we have here the serious possibility that human beings can be first causes of some of what they do.

I have shown earlier in this book why it is most reasonable to regard people as first causes. I began by arguing why there is no philosophical and scientific justification for thinking this impossible. Then I argued in what sense people are free—in what sense they have the capacity to make original choices, to take the initiative in producing some events in nature.

The usual attitude today is that the only way we could imagine this is by conceiving nature as irrational; existentialists (and, as we have seen, some scientists, too) tend to move in that direction when they defend human freedom of choice.

Theists do, of course, defend free will, but their approach does not offer an alternative to Hayek's position, one that is addressed to problems in a naturalistic, scientific manner (broadly conceived), in contrast to a supernaturalistic, ineffable, or mystical approach.

When free will is suggested to social scientists, the response is usually a dogmatic declaration that it is scientifically impossible. This, however, is not a scientific conclusion but a philosophical dogma.[25] It is worth noting why the rejection of free will is taken to be important

25. Machan, *The Pseudo-Science of B. F. Skinner*, pp. 26–28; 62–65.

within social science circles. Most of contemporary social science is either Humean or Kantian—broadly, the division between positivists and Weberians. No doubt there are now other developments. But within these, it is required that each instance of a cause should have (in the last analysis) events or occurrences as its constituents. Any explanation of something in nature, including society, must end by citing some event as the cause. (The slight variation introduced by recent theorists indebted to positivism is the term "variable." But a variable or a factor is still, in the last analysis, an event, some motion in time and space.) Human beings, however, are individual entities, not events (even if events take place within such entities). As human beings it would then be impossible to be a cause of anything. Thus to remain scientific as conceived in this philosophical framework, free will must be denied a priori.

Within the alternative scheme I am proposing it is an open question whether people are free or not, for on ontological or metaphysical grounds it is possible that they are. I shall not again defend free will here.[26] The basic argument for it is that the prospect of knowing what is true (including what is true about the free-will issue) and of distinguishing it from falsehood requires the freedom of the person making the evaluation. Rationality is itself inconceivable without freedom of the will. Furthermore, most of us are able to identify whether specific actions are free, forced, accidental, or as yet unexplained. It may help here to reflect on the tortuous evidential procedures required in criminal trials so as to demonstrate that a defendant is not responsible for his actions. The defendant bears the burden of proof of lack of capacity, which indicates that in some institutions the causal efficacy of

---

26. In addition to my earlier efforts, see also Nathaniel Branden, *The Psychology of Self-Esteem* (Los Angeles: Nash, 1969); Tibor R. Machan, *The Pseudo-science of B.F. Skinner;* Edward Madden and Rom Harre, "In Defense of Natural Agents," *Philosophical Quarterly* (April 1973): 117–32. For a very interesting approach to the issue, see also Edward Pols, *Mind Regained* (Ithaca, N.Y.: Cornell University Press, 1998).

human beings is accepted as the norm, whereas incapacity is taken to be special. Hayek, incidentally, regards human causal efficacy as part of a deterministic view of human affairs that, however, lacks the needed scientific support. He does admit that there may be philosophical objections to determinism other than those he advances.

To deny the identification of free actions on a priori grounds would betray an unjustified loyalty to empiricism and the intersubjectivist doctrine of objective knowledge. This is not to say that to identify whether some behavior is self-determined or caused by some other agency is a simple matter. Sometimes it may be, although to prove that it is so could be difficult in any case. But that problem arises in any instance of identification. It needs to be noted that I have not made it my task here to demonstrate the existence of free actions on anyone's part. I would argue, however, that a correct analysis of human action must regard the latter as free to be action at all. So, in a sense, if we have evidence of innumerable instances, as well as results, of human action, then the case for freedom is overwhelming.

I suggest a point at which a form of spontaneity enters the present scheme. In human affairs one can be free, fundamentally, in that one's mind is free to judge and guide conduct. But a judgment of the nature and the guidance of conduct would best be conceived along the following lines. The process of obtaining the grounds for the conclusion that something is so is an active, not a passive, one—a person might voluntarily or without external stimulus activate his or her capacity of being aware and form conceptual knowledge and understanding by means of that action. Or, to put it differently, one can look, see, and think things over, put two and two together. The process is active, not passive.

Human rationality, when exercised, is an activity conducted in accordance with valid reasoning, but it is not a static deductive process. So when it is argued that man is a rational animal, it is unwarranted to infer that human beings are therefore simply machines capable of performing calculations, however much that may be part of what they can do. It would be more accurate to think of human beings as capable of activating a faculty the operations of which are most fruitfully carried out in accordance with sound principles. I am talking in a philosophical vein, but in ordinary life we seem to think of people along these lines anyway. Even economists convinced that people act only to satisfy desires or psychologists who conceive of human behavior as governed by laws of operant behavior engage in arguments to try to persuade their colleagues, if not their wives, husbands, children, and political representatives.

Again, if what I have said is right, then spontaneity and rationality are indeed very closely related. One could argue that since a free and rational person is one who engages in clear thinking, the imprisoned, rigid person is one who relies on what others say, on what his culture gives him, on what he has picked up—without ever paving his own way.

So we have here a conception of spontaneity and rationality that conflicts with Hayek's. Reason is on the side of freedom, indeed inextricably tied to it. And, contrary to Hayek, it is those who try to plan the individual's life who incur the burden of antirationalism. They are stifling human reason—preventing the society's rational solutions to problems, forming rational organizations, and developing a rational order, one that is appropriate to us as rational beings.

FREEDOM AND VALUES

One problem with discussing values nowadays is that the majority of intellectuals and scientists construe values as necessarily antinatural or supernatural. If there is a theory of value that appeals to social scientists, it is utilitarianism. But the utilitarian theory is embedded in the empiricist framework and has the resulting difficulties of locating value in that which is open to sensory observation. Pleasures, pains, economic need, and the like figure as plausible candidates for the assignment of value or disvalue within such a theory. But most people see this result as inadequate. The first objection is that although some of the obvious benefits and disadvantages that people possess or might acquire can be observed, others cannot. Empiricism does well with pain and pleasure, with profit and loss, with benefit versus cost, or with efficiency versus inefficiency—these have observable features within the various contexts in which they are discussed and treated. But from the early days of hedonism, of which utilitarianism is clearly a relative, identifying the higher profits and losses, the goods and evils of human life, raised epistemological problems. The finer pleasures, the profound pains—happiness and degradation—are not easy to locate by sensory observation, physical measurement, and the like.

Two stances have usually been taken in the face of these difficulties. Some have insisted that no higher or finer pleasures, no noble ideas or values, and no profound miseries or evils exist—instead, we are facing mythical notions similar to "demon" or "witch" or "angel." Others have accepted a radical dualism and, although asserting that values exist, have rejected them as incapable of being rationally understood. I am not certain where Hayek stood on these alternatives—I suspect he fell between the two categories. His willingness to talk about values, his merely occasional or rare suggestion of specific instances, and his skepticism about anyone's capacity to identify any give evidence of a disregard of values. Yet he also invoked the language of ideals and values in his writing, so it is not easy to place him.

These, however, are not the only alternatives. I have focused on them because they are prominent within the Anglo-American tradition as influenced by Hume and Kant. Humeans would, as I see it, take the alternative of explaining away values as objects of sociological inquiry, whereas Kantians would relegate them to the supernatural in the well-known Kantian dualism of the practical versus the moral.

When we depart from this tradition and turn to Continental philosophy after Kant, we see another alternative. This is to reconcile values with facts by way of Marxist scientific socialism. Marx wanted to incorporate values into his science, and he attempted this by way of dialectics. As in Plato, so in Marx dialectics points to perfection, to nature's fullest realization. But in Plato this remained at the epistemological level—dialectical reasoning led to knowledge of perfect natures. With Hegel and Marx, nature itself engaged in dialectical development, striving through revolutionary leaps for the resolution of all strife and contradiction.

In Marxism values are what nature's end holds in store for us. Communism is the fullest realization of humankind, so that at present we must be conceived of as children moving toward maturity. The greatest value in this culmination of the historical dialectic is equality—all human beings will fully exhibit the essential nature of man. All Marxist-oriented criticism of present-day affairs rests on the future value of human equality. An understanding of that future yields all of history's rationale as well.

The Marxist egalitarian scheme at least appears to provide a satisfactory resolution of the fact-value dichotomy. Reason and goodness have merged, and the rational and good society is egalitarian. Everything done to help history to achieve that goal is both rational and good.[27] I am not holding, of course, that the Marxist scheme is valid. What I am saying is that it fulfills a need for those interested in solving a problem that actually faces us. It promises a solution of the fact-value problem, and for that reason alone it gains attention. Since it is also a comprehensive doctrine, covering all the bases with metaphysical, epistemological, ethical, political, and aesthetic components, it has a staying power beyond that provided by positivism, existentialism, or the Hayekian system.

One may say that nature abhors a vacuum and that fools rush in where wise men fear to tread. There is a vacuum in value theory in the current Anglo-American intellectual atmosphere, and Marxism tried to fill it. As with the thirsty who will drink poisoned water rather than

27. Machan, *Human Rights and Human Liberties*, pp. 250–51.

face sure death from thirst, we may interpret the pervasive and persistent clutching at the Marxist alternative as a sign of the philosophical bankruptcy of our age. This is a large and ambitious point, but I am confident that some of what I have said will call to mind evidence to support it enough that we can reflect on the matter seriously.

Given the earlier considerations, I can now suggest that Marxism is not the solution. The value-oriented approach is quite compatible with Hayek's concern for liberty—even required for it. If human nature means being a purposive thinking agent, and if we are unique for having to *choose* to pursue the values and practice the virtues suited to our lives, then political liberty is a necessary condition of a flourishing, successful, or morally proper human life. This is naturalistic in that political liberty is somewhat like water to a fish, a need for the sort of life appropriate for the being involved. Liberty is a necessary but insufficient condition of human excellence. It is because each person should strive to succeed as the kind of being he is that each person must be free of others' interference with him. Liberty is indeed a value, man's political value, a good that each person in society requires by nature, a natural right.

Hayek has come close to saying that liberty and ethics are in opposition: "Isn't the idea that society or the political area is bound to ethics, a view of what is right for man, almost incompatible with the idea that a man ought to have freedom?"[28] This is a mistake, however. If there is a system of ethics that is naturally right for human beings, and if this system justifies political liberty for human beings in their social situations, then without the admission of that ethical system one is unable to give liberty normative support. As an instance, who could deny that in any society some people are destitute? Plans designed to remedy such situations may not be supported by knowledge we should

28. Tibor R. Machan, "Economics, Politics and Freedom: An Interview with F. A. Hayek," *Reason* (February 1975): 4–12. See, however, chapter 4, note 12, for a different view from Hayek.

ideally like to have, but is this sufficient reason for giving up the plans? Even after a long history of ineffectual social planning, only with a sound normative objection to planning or social engineering can we rationally expect such programs to be abandoned. The mere limitation of human knowledge is not a sufficient ground for discontinuing the attempts to reach the goals of social engineering. In short, why should a political system admit liberty as a highest goal? Unless this can be answered with reference to an ethical system that is universalizable, the normative case of liberty is lost. And without it, there are the problems, discussed earlier, with something like Hayek's naturalistic evolutionary position.

Yet the worry of many defenders of the free society, Hayek among them, has been that reliance on an ethical system to justify liberty would necessarily undercut the latter. For if we know what is right for someone, must we not impose it upon him? From the fact, however, that human beings ought to live in such and such a manner, it simply does not follow that anyone is justified in forcing them to do so. Indeed, if the philosophical slogan "Ought implies can" is correct for ethical principles, as I think it is, then the imposition of conformity to moral edicts does not produce anything like moral conduct. Such conduct must be chosen. So the logical force of ethical skepticism as against authoritarianism vanishes, *pace* Hayek (*and* Milton Friedman).

Moreover, it seems that in certain contexts the skeptical defense of the free society can be an obstacle rather than a benefit to the realization of such a political situation. Leo Strauss points out:

> Generous liberals view the abandonment of natural right not only with placidity but with relief. They appear to believe that our inability to acquire any genuine knowledge of what is intrinsically good or right compels us to be tolerant of every opinion about good or right or to recognize all preferences or all "civilizations" as equally respectable. Only unlimited tolerance is in accordance with reason. But this leads to the admission of a rational or natural right of every preference that is tolerant of other preferences or, negatively ex-

pressed, of a rational or natural right to reject or condemn all intolerant or all "absolutist" positions. The latter must be condemned because they are based on a demonstrably false premise, namely, that men can know what is good. . . . But there is a tension between the respect for diversity or individuality and the recognition of natural right. When liberals became impatient of the absolute limits to diversity or individuality that are imposed even by the most liberal version of natural right, they had to make a choice between natural right and the uninhibited cultivation of individuality. They chose the latter. Once this step was taken, tolerance appeared as one value or ideal among many, and not intrinsically superior to its opposite. In other words, intolerance appeared as a value equal in dignity to tolerance. But it is practically impossible to leave it at the equality of all preference or choices. If the unequal rank of choices cannot be traced to the unequal rank of their objectives, it must be traced to the unequal rank of the acts of choosing; and this means eventually that genuine choice, as distinguished from spurious or despicable choice, is nothing but resolute or deadly serious decision. Such a decision, however, is akin to intolerance rather than to tolerance. Liberal relativism has its roots in the natural-right tradition of tolerance or in the notion that everyone has a natural right to the pursuit of happiness as he understands happiness, but in itself it is a seminary of intolerance.[29]

I believe that anyone aware of conditions prevalent in our culture and world today cannot fail to appreciate Strauss's point. It seems clear that the logic of the skeptical, relativist approach has allowed the victory of the antilibertarian political forces in our age. They are the serious, vehement, indignant groups and their intellectual representatives; they are the so-called radical professors, the third-world spokesmen, the Ralph Naders, the bombers, the John N. Grays, and the leaders of the radical feminist rallies with their obvious desire for power and obvious disdain for liberty.

29. Leo Strauss, *Natural Right and History* (Chicago: University of Chicago Press, 1953), p. 65.

It seems to me, then, that values and liberty are not in fundamental conflict. Quite to the contrary. But more important, value and liberty are logically connected, since political liberty is the necessary condition of human beings' pursuit of correct values. Admittedly, it is only when individuals take the initiative to do so that we have both the necessary and the sufficient conditions of human excellence. But here is one of the most profound insights of the libertarian tradition—that people cannot be made good and that the state is the least capable agent for achieving that goal because it must demoralize culture whenever it wields power, it must rob people of the opportunity to exercise their capacity for being moral agents.

IT'S NOT ABOUT THE CONCLUSIONS!

In the end the difference between Hayek's views and those offered for consideration here is negligible in respect of their conclusions. First, there is no denigration of science in my approach but a suggestion that certain victories won the scientific way really may have been won by a combination of philosophical movements, science, politics, morality, and other developments in human history. It is arguable that the potential for the scientific revolution has existed since the works of Aristotle were translated from the Arabic and that the real substance of that revolution was political. This political element in turn had to do with renewed confidence in the human capacity to improve life. Some unjustified conclusions may have been carelessly drawn from this, as Hayek himself points out in several places. But the self-assertiveness of human beings is not itself bad, nor something without which pure methodological advances could produce much in the way of progress.

To get to more specialized points, consider Hayek's case against planning. He rests it on the uncertainty about what suits individuals' lives and the lack of capacity to predict what individuals will do—in short, the lack of knowledge needed for a plan. All this may be so, but planners are notoriously willing to take risks, especially with the lives of others. Perhaps, they seem to say, just this once, we can succeed, even after years of failure. So let us charge ahead with another program of regulations and plans. Of course, we don't know enough, but isn't life itself a risk? Don't businesspeople act in the face of uncertainty? Why should government not do so?

The answer is that it is morally wrong, that it contradicts the value of liberty. Individuals should enjoy liberty because it is naturally right for them in a social context—their moral nature cannot flourish without it. Planners should plan their own lives, for here is where they have moral authority. Hayek's demonstration of the planners' incapacity supports this point. Obviously the prospects of living better are greater when people attend to their own circumstances, because they are in a better position to know what they require. The kind of conception of human mind I outlined earlier renders it highly probable, though certainly not guaranteed, that free individuals will make better decisions and the entire systems will be more rational than one in which the few try to accomplish that which they cannot do—namely, learning the limits of suitable conduct and aspirations for all.

But it is wrong even to suggest that planning is the rational way whereas the lack of planning is somehow the result of skepticism. We know that a free system is better, more productive, more suitable for human beings. The planners are mostly ill-equipped. Yet there are a few here and there who make a right decision once in a while—as when they look closely to find out and order, like competent doctors, some remedy that works. From this the entire system is fed with confidence. Unless even that instance of good judgment is condemned as wrong because it results at the expense of liberty, the planners can go on with moral legitimacy on their side.

We might recall here Hayek's idea that deliberate planning should enforce very general laws. In short, his conception and endorsement of the rule of law also gain support from the present perspective. Human nature is such that each person is similar to others in some respects and differs from most in the rest. So human societies work when laws refer to general needs and capacities, those shared by all people. All are purposive agents, and it is naturally right for them to have their freedom protected and preserved. Beyond that there should be greater and greater diversity. This does not mean that there is not a right conception of happiness that escapes Strauss's charge of relativism. It is simply that although one can know what another's happiness is, it is in the nature of the moral life that no one can make another happy in the strict and relevant sense of that phrase. One can even conceive of how another might achieve that happiness—one can write it down, dramatize it, even offer advice. But that is different from producing it for the other, and not just because of the wide variety of modes of happiness or goodness possible for human individuals.[30]

So here again Hayek's points are essential to showing the prospects of liberty, for indeed people are more favorably positioned to achieve their own moral self-realization and proper self-actualization than others would be, especially those who sit in governmental seats of power. But this does not mean that once in a while some people cannot know what is right.

It is to be hoped that these few points will show why I believe it important to study and understand Hayek's work. But what I have said also indicates that his work is insufficient. His case for liberty is not powerful enough to solve problems that any political theory must face.

30. For more on this, see Tibor R. Machan, *Classical Individualism* (London: Routledge, 1998).

CHAPTER SIX

Do Ideas
Matter?

WHEN IDEAS ARE SEEN AS FRUITLESS

In this final chapter I focus on a particularly crucial implication of the denial of human initiative, one that has had such a powerful impact on the social sciences. The effects of this idea on some areas of modern society have already been explored—for example, whether the idea of a victim makes any sense and whether political liberty can be rendered coherent if determinism is true.

The implication of determinism I discuss here is the inefficacy of ideas. Do ideas have the power of producing anything in the world? Does what we think amount to a productive process or is it merely something of a link between some events and what we do?[1]

The implication that ideas do not matter is evident in the writings of some materialists, including Thomas Hobbes and Ludwig Feuerbach, but they do not make the point explicitly. Karl Marx, of course, did almost admit outright that as far as he understood human beings,

---

1. For a somewhat different approach to this issue, see chapter 9, "Entrepreneurship," in James E. Chesher and Tibor R. Machan, *The Business of Commerce: Examining an Honorable Profession* (Stanford, Calif.: Hoover Institution Press, 1999).

they had no capacity for initiating ideas—their ideas emerged in response to their involvement with the material world. This is Marx's famous economic determinism.

Few realize, however, that non-Marxist determinism also leads to the denial of the efficacy of human thinking, of ideas as a force to reckon with in reality. The widespread scientism of our era—whereby everything in the universe has to conform to the laws governing the behavior of matter-in-motion—left us with a legacy of the passive human mind; indeed, the passive human individual. B. F. Skinner's promulgation of this view does make the impotence of ideas explicit.[2] And it is arguable that the widespread belief in the victimized status of nearly everyone in our era is due, in large measure, to this doctrine of essential human passivity, even as the very idea of a victim, as we have discussed before, lacks coherent meaning in such a framework.

What is not often acknowledged is that this passive view of human nature is most prominently embraced by some of the most fervent defenders of political-economic liberty, namely, certain scientific economists.[3]

Classical and neoclassical economic science had emerged from the ubiquitous scientism of the modern era. The discipline rests, in large measure, on the belief that human behavior can be explained the way the behavior of any material substance may be, namely, by reference to causes acting on—or variables affecting—the agent, who then reacts in kind. Although most contemporary economists eschew talk of causes, just as do most scientists, and substitute the formalism of mathematical model building and the language of dependent and independent variables, the basic idea remains the same. Human beings act because they must.

This is in part a response to the dualistic and idealistic positions

2. See B. F. Skinner, *Science and Human Behavior* (New York: Macmillan, 1953).

3. Tibor R. Machan, *Capitalism and Individualism: Reframing the Argument for the Free Society* (New York: St. Martin's Press, 1990).

of some of the most influential ancient and medieval philosophies and theologies. The slowly developing attitude that much of scientific economics has come to embrace is this: If the conception of human beings as free moral agents does not permit taking commerce and business seriously—if these are ruled out of court by the dominant school of morality—then let us abandon the moral point of view entirely. Let us, instead, conceive of the pursuit of profit or prosperity as natural drives no one can escape. In short, we are to be seen as constant maximizers. From this it turns out that ideas really have no role in our lives because we will do just exactly what we must.

Today this view is combined with neo-Darwinism of a certain kind—for example, that of Richard Dawkins, in his book *The Selfish Gene*[4]—to pretty much deny any causal role for human ideas in the world.

THE ECONOMIC WAY OF THINKING

In particular, when we study economics, we learn that a central idea dominates this social science: that people are motivated to maximize their utilities. Another way of saying this is to say that people are necessarily selfish. We have already noted a portion of what Milton Friedman said about this but let us now look at the entire remark more carefully: "every individual serves his own private interest. . . . The great Saints of history have served their 'private interest' just as the most money grubbing miser has served his interest. The *private interest* [italics in original] is whatever it is that drives an individual."[5]

One implication that has been drawn from this view is that everything that happens is the result of human beings naturally and necessarily pursuing their rational self-interest. Such a belief argues, in

4. London: Oxford University Press, 1976.
5. Milton Friedman, "The Line We Dare Not Cross," *Encounter* (November 1976): 11.

effect, that ideas do not matter at all, that when we teach people, present to them arguments and theories, especially concerning what they ought to do, this will have no impact on them because they will just do whatever is in their rational self-interest.

This psychological egoistic position has some devastating consequences for the teaching of ethics, in part because it denies the reality of human choice in the bringing about of actions and what these actions will aim for, what will be their purpose. For example, it renders irrelevant all efforts to urge people in the business community to consider ethical issues, including problems of discrimination, honest dealings, destruction of the environment, conscientious treatment of employees or customers, responsibility to the quality of the community, and so forth. No appeal to the mind or the conscience of members of the business community can ever be effective. The best that can be done is to feed people in business the information that will help facilitate the pursuit of their "private interest." Unless their self-interest is evidently enhanced, nothing can be expected in the way of change of policy.

In this discussion, however, I will not focus on business ethics as such. Suffice it to say that the more popular efforts to assess the ethics of business practices are misguided.[6] Contrary to mainstream teachings in that field, the pursuit of profit—that is, broadly speaking, striving to prosper in life—is morally proper, so long as it does not occur at the expense of others' rights and adheres to ordinary decency (involving trust, honesty, courtesy, industry, and similar virtues). Indeed, commerce and the profession of business are motivated by the

6. For more on this, see Chesher and Machan, *The Business of Commerce.* Just how widespread the view is that business or commerce requires no attention to morality is illustrated by what billionaire George Soros told CBS-TV's *60 Minutes* program on December 20, 1998, namely, that when he acts as a business agent, he is "amoral," whereas otherwise he acts morally.

Such a dichotomization of human agency stems, in part, from the view that social sciences such as economics require seeing people as automatons.

virtue of prudence, the need to take good care of oneself and one's intimates. People are not automatically, instinctively "self-interested," as many in the field of economics claim. We all need to learn to serve our best interest, and good business exemplifies such learning even when misunderstood to be something else, such as automatic utility maximization.

Be that as it may, however, it is my task in this chapter to consider the broader and more troublesome idea advanced by some economists, namely, whether ideas can influence the conduct of people—whether, to put it bluntly, ideas can have consequences—especially in the sphere of politics.

DEFINING OUR TERMS

By "politics" or "public affairs" I mean a sphere of activity of concern to all those involved in community life (e.g., vis-à-vis their participation in such community life). For some—Marxists, for instance—this includes everything as the public realm. For some—classical liberals—it is a limited, specific sphere.

Politics (lawmaking and enforcement)—or the public sphere—is distinctive in that it must involve the use of force upon persons who may at the time when it occurs find it very objectionable (even if their actions may be said to have invited it). It is the only realm with that distinction—in medicine, science, education, or commerce, for instance, using force is never deemed justified without the express agreement of those on whom it is used.

Ideologies are reasonably integrated outlooks on reality, or at least on human social life. I do not mean, as Marxists do, facades of theories serving to rationalize one's preexisting objectives and the best means for achieving them. (Oddly, this characterization is only a bit different from how some neoclassical economic types understand ideology, namely "ideas that serve one's interest.") Rather I accept the common-sense notion that ideologies are reasonably simple and integrated sets of ideas addressed to facilitate an understanding and navigation of human social life.

ARGUING FOR IDEAS

Arguing for the efficacy of political ideas is just a bit odd. The influence of a Karl Marx, a Lenin, a Thomas Jefferson, a Milton Friedman, and others might make it superfluous. Even to advance an argument on the topic would appear to make its point well enough.

Suppose I convinced some bureaucrat that ideas do not matter. But then would not the significance of ideas have been demonstrated anyway? My thesis would have helped lead someone to follow certain procedures and to avoid others. This person would possibly avoid reading any letters proposing new ideas to his or her boss, thinking these to be irrelevant, opting for flipping a coin before choosing, thus making decisions randomly.

Yet within the liberal tradition especially—starting with Hobbes and including Hume, Smith, and more contemporary thinkers such as George Stigler—the fundamental power of ideas is often denied. The commitment to science, based on the model of classical mechanics, has often inclined such thinkers to claim that material factors, not thoughts, are the main moving force in human affairs. (This is not far from Marx's own economic determinism, interestingly enough.)

WHY MIGHT IDEAS BE IMPOTENT?

Now we can ask, Why is there a problem about the power of ideas? As a start, consider that for David Hume, a main figure in the liberal tradition, reason and ideas are "the slave of the passions." Before ideas, there is already the urge, drive, or motive to seek something. Our theories merely express the best strategy to reach our goals. We are driven, and we, who possess large brains, think up ideas and establish institutions that serve our goals. Aristotle, in contrast, thought reason guided the passions—one's emotions emerged in response to one's implicit or explicit judgment as to what is right, good, beautiful, healthy, wise, significant, tragic, and so forth. Knowledge of the fierceness of the bear leads to fear of bears. Knowledge of the value of a friend and friendship leads us to rejoice when our friends visit. Knowledge of the value of our goals leads us to devise suitable institutions and practices to pursue them.

For Aristotle and his followers, ideology or philosophy is a set of ideas that could be true or false. We could, in turn, learn of this and be guided to act in line with what we have learned. Ideas range from the most minute to the most gigantic abstractions that we sometimes take to guide our conduct—notions as to whether we should eat foods containing much or little fat, what our children deserve from us, our concepts of right and wrong, good and bad, beautiful and ugly, truth and falsity, the value of liberty or equality as social ideas, and so forth.

In the following section I speak in favor of this last tradition in our intellectual history.

IDEAS AND THE ECONOMIST

George Stigler and others, following Hume and Hobbes, have argued that ideas actually have no influence on the way the human world works. Stigler's paper, "Do Economists Matter?"[7] argues that view.

---

7. George Stigler, *The Economist as Preacher and Other Essays* (Chicago: University of Chicago Press, 1982). In contrast, consider the following understanding of the ways of ideas: "political philosophy, when it has an impact on the world, affects the world only indirectly, through the gradual penetration, usually over generations, of questions and arguments from abstruse theoretical writings into the consciousness and the habits of thought of educated persons, and from there into political and legal arguments and eventually into the structure of alternatives among which political and practical choices are actually made." (Thomas Nagel, "Justice, Justice, Shalt Thou Pursue: The Rigorous Compassion of John Rawls," *New Republic*, October 25, 1999, pp. 36–37.)

Furthermore, in his Adam Smith Lecture[8] he even holds that all government policies are utility maximizing. Utility maximization is something we all do automatically. And government, in democracies at least, does our bidding, regardless of good ideas to the contrary. (Accordingly Stigler opined, on the *MacNeil–Lehrer News Hour* [fall 1988] that it also makes no difference who wins that year's presidential election.) Not only is it the case that, *pace* John Maynard Keynes and F. A. Hayek, what economists teach has no impact on the world of commerce and government, neither do the convictions of political leaders serve any such purpose.

So what does have influence? Market forces do—the productive efforts, demands, and availability of resources manifest on the market. What people desire, what others will do to satisfy those desires, and how much material there is with which to do this—all this matters; the rest is epiphenomena, a mere sideshow.

Actually, in another paper[9] Stigler tries to avoid denigrating scientists. He says, "Please do not read into my low valuation of professional preaching a similarly low valuation of scientific work."[10] This is because "Once a general relationship in economic phenomena is discovered and verified, it becomes a part of the working knowledge of everyone."[11]

This idea, also tried by Marx—namely, in his attempt to exempt himself from the passive followers of workers' and bourgeois's impulses—is interesting but ultimately inconsistent. Stigler says that "Man is eternally a utility maximizer, in his home, in his office—be it public or private—in his church, in his scientific work, in short every-

---

8. George Stigler, "The Effect of Government on Economic Efficiency," *Business Economics* 23 (January 1988): 7–13.

9. George Stigler, "Economics and Ethics," *The Essence of Stigler* (Stanford, Calif.: Hoover Institution Press, 1986).

10. Ibid., p. 35.

11. Ibid.

where."[12] If so, why trust the scientists to remain objective with the material he passes off as scientific discovery? Why hope that his findings will become general knowledge? Why should scientists not merely pursue what suits their self-interest, be that truth, falsehood, acceptance, popularity, self-deception, political power, or whatnot? Or, alternatively, if we do trust the scientist, why not other "preachers" of alleged truths? Why not philosophers or moral theorists? What disqualifies them? I return to this last issue later.

Stigler's position is an elaboration of the Hobbesian-Humean-Smithian doctrine about the real forces operating in human society. (That itself shows that ideas have considerable influence. They certainly have influenced George Stigler's scholarly behavior.) All these ideas are derivative of the scientific tradition that propounds that everything in nature—everything knowable by us, at least—is composed of matter-in-motion. So the sciences of human social life, especially economics, actually concern principles of physical behavior. (Marx, too, held this view; but he was a dialectical, not a mere reductive materialist.)

If ideas at least have this kind of impact—namely, if they can be shown to influence how theorists think about the world, what they write, and what they teach in their classrooms—why not grant also that scholars—for example, Henry Kissinger, Walter Heller, or Milton Friedman—can have an impact on public policy when they preach not methodology, epistemology, or philosophy of science but fiscal policy? And don't those Chicago graduates—for example, Chilean finance minister Hernan Buchi, who convinced the Chilean ruler, General Augusto Pinochet, to be at least permissive toward Chile's commercial sector—also influence economic matters? Why not go even further and admit that the Chicago graduates sitting at the various branches of the Federal Reserve are making something of an

---

12. George Stigler, *The Economist as Preacher and Other Essays*, p. 35.

impact? Or that Adam Smith and John Maynard Keynes influenced policy makers?

Stigler's position, on first inspection, defeats itself—at least if one ascribes any potency to it at all. Some of Stigler's students and admirers have clearly been influenced by his views on this topic, to the extent that they teach it in their classrooms and lead some of their students to take it seriously enough to inject it into their papers in my own philosophy classes. They learn these ideas from such teachers as Robert Ekelund in the Department of Economics at Auburn University, for example. His *Mercantilism as a Rent-Seeking Society*[13] is certainly influenced by Stigler's ideas. And although any one such case may not be much, a good bit of it here and there amounts to something important in the development of a society.

Even though, as we have seen, the case in favor of a free-market system of economics rests, in part, on the fact—if it is a fact—that human beings can take the initiative in such matters as changing the laws of a society. How else could we make sense of the idea that teaching the value of the free market could well make a difference to the economic system of a society, consisting, in part, of laws of property, contract, international trade, and so forth.

It is worth noting, also, that Stigler and his disciples refer to market forces that determine events in the social world. But for them these include the ideas that may have an influence on public affairs. Should they lump together all social forces as market forces? Some ideas as social forces lead to mere micro events, others to enormous changes within the body politic and even in markets.

I am reasonably sure that such dialectical or reflexive (logical) moves carry little weight with materialists (reductivists). They tend to stick to the view that genuine knowledge—including explanation and understanding of human social life—is only available by way of the methods they have extrapolated from classical mechanics. Still, it

13. College Station: Texas A&M Press, 1981.

might be useful to discuss this, at least for the benefit of those who are watching the discussion from the sidelines and have not yet made up their minds.

PUBLIC CHOICE THEORY

The place where the Hobbes-Hume-Stigler thesis has become especially prominent in our time is in public choice theory. This theory says that, starting with standard economic assumptions, it is possible to explain public affairs. To quote James Buchanan, "Politicians and bureaucrats are seen as ordinary persons, and 'politics' is viewed as a set of arrangements, a game if you will, in which many players with quite disparate objectives interact so as to generate a set of outcomes that may not be either internally consistent or efficient."[14] In other words, in the realm of politics, as in the market, within certain rules all parties aspire toward their own utility maximization.

Why is this interesting enough to warrant formation of a new school of applied economics, a journal, and even the Nobel Prize (which Buchanan received in 1986)?

The idea is basically this: Many of us have, supposedly naively, thought that public officials have the distinctive job of serving the public, not their private interests. But that is apparently an error. Indeed, it seems that they cannot do other than pursue their private interests. As we saw at the start of this discussion, Milton Friedman tells us, in more general terms, that the one motive of all action is self or private interest.[15] Or in Stigler's view, as we have seen, "Man is eternally a utility maximizer."[16]

The teaching of public choice theory, however, is very misleading when read with the facility of the normal English-speaking reader.

14. *New York Times*, October 16, 1986.
15. Friedman, "The Line We Dare Not Cross."
16. Stigler, *The Economist as Preacher*, p. 35.

"Private interest" in everyday discourse is a concept used to distinguish one set of concerns—something on the person's mind, some goal or objective—that a person may have from others. As such, a private interest centers on the welfare, advantage, or benefit of the acting agent. In contrast, the public interest designates concerns that are of benefit to every member of one's community. This may even include matters not of benefit—at times perhaps of disadvantage—to the person pursuing the public interest. Such a person, at least ideally, would be a politician or bureaucrat, for example.

In contrast, within the public choice framework, following Friedman's basic premise, the concept "interest" amounts to "anything of concern to someone." This concern may be focused on personal benefits or on the welfare of neighbors, of total strangers, or of everyone. So "private interest" designates whatever is of concern to someone. It does not mean whatever benefits the agent. Nor does it mean, as some often suggest, what the agent believes benefits him or her. Even that assumes that objective criteria may be invoked to distinguish real from apparent benefits to agents.

Once we fully appreciate the above points, a strictly interpreted, universalizable version of public choice theory no longer says something unusual but only something tautological. At least this is so if one takes it that public choice theory fully explains or renders intelligible political events, which is clearly its ambition.

Of course, public choice theory has been very useful in understanding political and bureaucratic behavior in the welfare state. That is because such a state treats its politicians and bureaucrats as promoters of various groups of vested interests—scientists, educators, artists, athletes, farmers, and all those who expect the government to provide them with support. This support, of course, is often defended as promoting the public interest, so as to render it more palatably justified as a government function. But any serious examination will discover that such use of the concept "public interest" or "public welfare" is confused, and misleading.[17]

Politicians and bureaucrats have disparate private objectives. Yet these may well include what we normally call the public interest, the welfare of the public at large, the common good, or justice at large. We can thus continue to think in our old-fashioned way. But we will need to choose new words, since the economist has expropriated the usual vocabulary that served us well to distinguish between, for example, a private entrepreneur and a public official.

THE ROLE OF IDEAS OR "IDEOLOGY"

One of the apparent implications of the strict versions of public choice theory and, more generally, of the economic approach to human behavior is that what drives our social affairs and institutions is not what we believe, not what we think, not our convictions and ideals, but merely our urges or passions. This is not how the point is put by the economic imperialists. They would argue, instead, that it is the maximization of utilities that drives each person and, therefore, the entire community wherever they are headed.

Here again the claim sounds quite outrageous, at least initially, prior to some of the caveats that are usually made. But if we take it at its most straightforward, questions spring to mind: Why should we study political economy, political philosophy, or even public choice theory? Why bother about understanding economic forces, the rate of inflation, "values," or morality? The economist's theory implies that none of this matters. What does matter is the inner drives, urges, impulses, instincts, or motives that actually underlie our actions. It is only our private interests that count—the force that drives us.

In commonsense terms, at least, this appears to be something

---

17. See Tibor R. Machan, *Private Rights and Public Illusions* (New Brunswick, N.J.: Transaction Books, 1995).

radical, even outlandish. Yet Stigler, we will recall, seems clearly enough to hold the above view. And I submit that the plausibility of it stems from how we would interpret the position in ordinary terms.

If what he means is that grand systems or theories do not usually directly shape ordinary life or supply and demand in existing markets or the sphere of day-to-day politics, he may be right enough. But no one denies this. At any given short period of human history, the impact of general ideas may be minuscule indeed. When during the cold war a conservative went shopping, only now and then did he or she consider that Chevron dealt with Marxist Angola and decide to purchase gasoline from some other outlet. Such decisions at the individual level have little impact. When they do, it is only because little of importance hinges on them—that is, when the cost is minimal.

And even when a chief executive officer (CEO) struggles in the world of commerce and considers whether to support import quotas, he or she is usually focused on how these policies will bear on the long-term profit potential of the firm. That, after all, is the CEO's job, not to mix his or her job description with a political role. Ideologically aware—not to mention motivated—CEOs are too few, as William Simon and Irving Kristol keep noticing in their frequent columns lamenting the fact, never mind that anyone who sees how wrong Karl Marx was about class consciousness might have warned them. The bourgeoisie is no less consistent and skillful in promoting its own rational self-interest than is the proletariat. So again Stigler's point holds, though probably not for his reasons.

However, in its own terms Stigler's point is too broad—indeed, tautological. He argues that not ideology but market forces have an impact. This sounds as if it were something of a discovery, an empirical finding achieved through research and study. Yet, once we see that for Stigler and his like-minded colleagues market forces include not just simple benefit and cost considerations made by members of the buying and voting public but ideology as well, the point no longer carries any factual content. Or, alternatively, since benefit and cost

considerations include the ideas that these members may find important to support or oppose, what Stigler and colleagues have ruled out
with one argument, they reintroduce with this broad conception of
market forces. Anything turns out to qualify as a market force: ideology, economic theory, religious ideals, and so forth.

IDEAS CAN HAVE CONSEQUENCES

As to whether ideas have consequence on public affairs, one can
point to the microbehaviors of various people and show that some,
however minuscule, consequences are clearly evident. But this suggests that a great deal more is possible. Many of us could come to
learn that a certain set of policies is immoral, wrong, or otherwise
unworthy of our support and worthy of our opposition. We could come
to act in line with this belief.

Indeed, most fundamentally, we implicitly and sometimes explicitly already do this. Every piece of human behavior is an action and
not just a piece of behavior precisely because there is a judgment that
gives that behavior its direction. As I turn off the light after I finish my
work in my office, I think of that plan—though not necessarily self-
consciously (I do not monitor myself so closely). I write my sentences
about ideology and public policy by thinking what I should say next,
what follows, and how I must meet objections. Then I undertake the
action of writing the sentence. And I am not some unusual being—
everyone does this. But many also act in ways that never come under
scrutiny—by mere habit, custom, or routine. These individuals are
not, however, without ideas. Their ideas are largely automatized—
acquired and accepted and then put to use without much supervision
by their second-order, intellectual, deliberate thinking.

So all public officials behave guided by certain ideas. The difference is that some keep tabs on their ideas, others do not, and others
do it in a perverse fashion—motivated not by a concern with truth but

with whether an idea plays well in Peoria or with the editors of the *New York Times.*

To deny that we are motivated by ideas—small ones, borrowed ones, scrutinized ones, and so forth—is paradoxical. Why would one do such a thing? How could one do so, when the distinctive aspect of human nature is just that we are thinking animals, not in possession of innate prompters or instincts, that drive us in the right direction? What would the point of ideas be if not to guide behavior—perhaps, in the case of George Stigler, to lead us to look at other factors in the marketplace than the ideas that permeate it.[18]

The lesson here is not too complicated: To avoid the nasty sting of the moralism of ancient and medieval thinking, some of the creative minds in the West have gone overboard and denied the very humanity of human beings. This seemed to be the only escape from the paradoxical doctrine that human beings, born on this earth and trying to flourish in their lives, nevertheless owed their lives to some supernatural dimension the pursuit of which required giving up the goods of this earth. If that is the price of morality, it would be best not to bother with it at all.

But this is another case of the proverbial "throwing out the baby with the bathwater." What we need is not a rejection but a revision of morality. We are unique because we guide ourselves with ideas. But these ideas must be carefully honed and not allowed to misguide us through fantasy and fright.

Instead of consigning our lives to chance, the forces over which we have no control, so as to gain a place in nature, it would be better to acknowledge our uniqueness and yet admit that this does not remove us from nature. It merely leaves it to us to adjust ourselves to the natural world prudently, and carefully, as well as prosperously and joyfully.

---

18. I explore some of these issues relating to the relationship between economics and ethics in greater detail in Machan, *Capitalism and Individualism.*

Of course, there is one very controversial implication that follows from all this. We are the kind of beings who must have room to make choices and commitments on our own. Regimenting us by either private criminals or oppressive governments amounts to violating our nature as free and responsible agents. This is the main public policy result of the fact that we are persons with the capacity to initiate our conduct and the responsibility to do it properly and virtuously. That, I believe, is also the unique and radical insight of the American political tradition as understood by most people who have looked to America as the country most hospitable to a flourishing human life.

Epilogue

WHAT HAS CONCERNED US in this book is whether human beings possess the capacity to initiate their conduct and what this implies for politics and public policy. There is no doubt here about limitations on our freedom to choose—the world around us imposes such limitations galore. Furthermore, we ourselves make commitments in terms of which we foreclose further choices in certain areas, such as marriage or contracting to write a book for someone.

There is also the plain fact that our own initiative functions in large part by taking what is available around us and putting it to our own use. Education, although involving vital doses of initiative, does so by our choice to grasp something, to infer from it something else, and so forth.

One reason that so many people find the determinist alternative palatable is that they confuse one's making use of what there is to learn, to mimic, or to revise as if those had themselves simply imposed upon us some information, conduct, or modification of belief. Why did we do X? Because of Y, where Y is some fact that could well bear upon our goals, aspirations, or concerns. Why did Johnny become a painter? His mother took him to many art galleries. This makes it appear that taking Johnny to art galleries made him into a painter.

Never mind that Johnny had to take the initiative to pay attention to the paintings. Of course, there had to have been paintings around to be heeded. But it is a mistake to give them the power to make Johnny into a painter. Without Johnny's initiative, the paintings would have continued to hang in the galleries without Johnny grasping them at all.

A similar analysis can be provided to all sorts of things that influence us—they are around and we can then pick and choose (or not pick and choose) them for our use. But they do not make us pick and choose them—we do that.

My focus here has not been on exactly how human initiative bears on all aspects of morality, although I have touched somewhat on that issue throughout the book. If we lack such initiative, ethics either is a bogus sphere or has to be drastically reconceived as behavior modification. (Even that will not work quite as we might think, for behavior modifiers would all be just doing what they are compelled to do by factors operating on them.) Morality requires initiative—to say you should or ought to do X means you can do it and it is right for you to choose it. It is, in turn, because of this that human beings require a type of community life wherein their right to choose is respected and protected, even if this also promotes less basic values such as knowledge, prosperity, innovation, and so forth.

Usually a work like this unavoidably leaves too much unsaid. Questions of detail surge to the mind as one reads positions stated in general terms. What about the role of mental illness in understanding human freedom? How about peer pressure, addiction, compulsions, obsessions, and the more subtle influences on us coming from our childhood histories, cultures, physical environments, and other elements of our living conditions?

These are all valid inquiries in connection with the place of free will or initiative in human life. Somewhat different ones face us, too—for example, do animals possess any free will at all? To what measure? How important is it for our understanding of their lives, and how we ought to treat them? (We sense, for example, that animals are not just machines we ought to treat arbitrarily, regardless of their pain and suffering. Is this because they have some measure of dignity, akin to what human beings possess?)

These and similar questions would occupy an even fuller treatment of our topic. Yet what needed to be done and what I aimed for here was a discussion of human initiative as a basic feature of our personal and community lives. Are we warranted in taking it seriously, and why so? And if so, what should we do about it regarding some of our basic institutions?

One need not be sentimental about this to appreciate that the human situation is fundamentally different from that of other living beings because we are free and thus carry moral responsibilities on how we live our lives. (Even those who urge us to heed the rest of nature because of its alleged intrinsic value testify to this when they address their pleas only to human beings!) It requires that we keep our thoughts, conduct, and institutions aligned to the fact of our freedom.

If we do, we will find that human beings will be able to live in accordance with their nature. Those who fail to heed this will, in turn, be scrutinized more and more strictly for failing to heed that we are ends in ourselves and not resources for even the most visionary purposes some of us may forge and wish us all to follow.

Our nature as free and responsible living beings is not the only vital fact about us, but it is very likely the most important. If it is not a myth, as many contend, then we should acknowledge it wherever human affairs are at stake.

INDEX

ABOUT THE AUTHOR

TIBOR R. MACHAN, professor emeritus at the department of philosophy, Auburn University, Alabama, is now Freedom Communications Professor and a fellow of the Leatherby Center on Entrepreneurship and Business Ethics at the Argyros School of Business and Economics at Chapman University, Orange, California. He is a research fellow at the Hoover Institution, Stanford, California, and public policy adviser to Freedom Communications, Inc., the *Orange County Register*'s family-owned parent company. A widely published columnist, his writing has appeared in the *Humanist, National Review, Barron's, The American Scholar*, and numerous daily newspapers throughout the country. Machan is author of twenty books, editor of another fifteen, and has written many scholarly papers. He edits *Reason Papers*, an annual journal of interdisciplinary normative studies. Machan lives in Silverado, California.

PHILOSOPHIC REFLECTIONS
ON A FREE SOCIETY

Business Ethics in the Global Market
Tibor R. Machan, editor

Education in a Free Society
Tibor R. Machan, editor

Morality and Work
Tibor R. Machan, editor